THE END OF 6%

THE END OF 6%

How to Get the Real Estate Expertise You Need
Without Paying Commission*

*Unless You Want To

Mollie W. Wasserman

ACRE® Publishing

Book Cover Design: Bill Earle of Accurance Inc.
Interior Design:Day to Day Enterprises
Editor: Shel Horowitz

ISBN-13: 978-0-9846111-3-3
ISBN-10: 0-9846111-3-4
10 9 8 7 6 5 4 3 2 1
Printed in the United States of America

Library of Congress Control Number: 2010911061

Publisher's Cataloging-in-Publication data
Wasserman, Mollie W.
    The end of 6% : how to get the real estate expertise you need without paying commission unless you want to / Mollie W. Wasserman.
    p. cm.
    Includes index.
    ISBN 978-0-9846111-3-3
1. Real estate business. 2. House buying. 3. House selling. 4. Home ownership. 5. Negotiation in business. I. The end of six percent : how to get the real estate expertise you need without paying commission unless you want to. II. Title.

HD259 .W37 2010
643/.12—dc22   2010922061

Published by ACRE® Publishing • Framingham, MA

This book is dedicated to nice folks who would like to get quality and value for their real estate dollar, while realizing the most profit when they buy or sell a home—as well as those folks who would like to have an avenue to get professional real estate counsel even if they're not looking to buy or sell.

and

All hard-working real estate professionals who strive every day to take the best care of their clients and who simply want to be paid fairly for their services, time, and the expertise that can only come from years of experience.

Warning

THIS BOOK WILL CHALLENGE MANY widely held myths about real estate. You will be exposed to the straight facts (and a lot of strong opinions), but absolutely no sales spiel. Those of us "in the trenches" have seen, over the years, where real estate value is won and where it is lost, where the public, responding to the hype put out by hucksters in misleading ads and sensational "news" articles, pick up pennies only to drop dollars. It's time that you, as a consumer, are honestly informed about the real workings of real estate, where and how to spend your hard-earned money, and where not to waste your energy and time.

It is also time for consumers, as well as the real estate industry, to begin regarding agents as the true professional consultants they are, rather than as salespeople simply selling a product to generate a sales commission.

When all is said and done, my passion and goal in writing this book is to get the word out that in real estate—as in other fiduciary fields such as finance and law–experience, knowledge, and expertise are not expensive—they are priceless.

Preface

I HAVE A SAYING TAPED TO MY DESK, right next to my computer that I look at almost daily:

> *God, grant me the strength to fight the good fight. Not because it's always winnable but because it needs to be fought.*

There's not a day that I read this verse when I don't immediately think of my dad and how, as I was growing up, he taught me through his example to "fight the good fight no matter the consequences."

It's this attitude that has led me to take on the sacred cows and hoary customs of the real estate industry: the "we've always done it that way" rigidity that serves the interests of neither the consumer nor the Realtor.

For the past 15 years, as I've experimented with different compensation options and a whole new way of looking at my industry, first as an individual practitioner, and later as a coach with ACRE® (the Accredited Consultant in Real Estate Program), I've heard my share of negative comments such as "Real estate has always been paid by commission," or "This is the way we've always done it."

Change is difficult and takes time. And changing an entire industry from paying real estate salespeople to move product, to paying them to provide counsel, guidance, and care to people looking to buy or sell their largest financial asset is, I believe, a fight that needs to be fought.

Is it winnable? Perhaps. But I hold no illusions that the "radical" ideas that I present in this book are going to be adopted by either the public or the real estate industry itself (at least in mass) in the near future. Shoot, they might not be adopted in my lifetime.

But as President John F. Kennedy said so eloquently in his inaugural address on January 20, 1961, when speaking of the many goals he wished our country to reach:

> *All this will not be finished in the first 100 days. Nor will it be finished in the first 1,000 days, nor in the life of this Administration, nor even perhaps in our lifetime on this planet. But let us begin.*

Acknowledgments

IT IS IMPOSSIBLE TO THANK EVERYONE who has contributed to my growth and therefore to making this book possible. Nevertheless, I will try.

To my editor and book shepherd, Shel Horowitz, who not only made my words sing, but also walked me through the process of bringing this book to fruition.

To Merv Forney, Judi Bryan, Ron Stuart and Paula Bean, for their tireless efforts in building the Accredited Consultant in Real Estate® (ACRE) Training and Certification program and for their contributions to this book.

In addition to Merv, Judi, Ron and Paula, to our growing army of pioneering ACRE®s and particularly, members of the ACRE® Board of Advisors: Stacy Erickson, Laurie Furem, Mary Pope-Handy, Vicki Lloyd, Tom Pickering, and Elwynn Schwartz for helping to bring the consulting model to hard-working REALTORS® everywhere

To Lisa Feldman, Dina Raneri, Betsy Robinson, Yolanda Evangelista, Margaret Rome, Heather Kamenelis, Karen Stefani, Tricia Radigan, and Donna Sines for their friendship.

Last, but certainly not least, I am forever grateful to my family.

To my husband, Steve, who has provided me the encouragement and support to reach for the stars—and who, in his own quiet way, has always been my biggest fan.

To my sons, Jeffrey and Daniel, who have each developed into very special young men. Thank you for keeping me grounded and constantly reminding me of what's important.

To my parents for teaching me that while a reputation can be won or lost in a day, one's good character is built over a lifetime. To my mom, Anita Woolf, for raising me to believe in myself even though my talents are quite different from hers. To my dad, Ken Woolf, for showing me through his example that it's okay to think "out of the box."

To my sisters, Sherri Noble and Lisa Ploss, who always have my back and are right in my corner.

To my in-laws, Reuben and Rosalind Wasserman, who have always shared with me the value in family.

And in loving memory of my grandparents:

To my grandmother, Jo Woolf, who, along with my mom, was always a testament to a woman's strength long before it was fashionable. And to my grandfather, Cy Woolf, who always called me his "rubber ball" in encouraging the resiliency of my character.

"Never doubt that a small group of thoughtful, committed people can change the world. Indeed, it is the only thing that ever has."
—*Margaret Mead*

"When the music changes, so does the dance."
—*African Proverb*

Table of Contents

Part 3: The Four Financial Potholes

Introduction

An Industry with an Identity Crisis

A FEW YEARS BACK, my friend and colleague, Lisa Feldman, mused this statement:

> You know, Mollie, I know we've talked about this before, but I'm finding it more and more difficult to get buyers to sign a buyer agency contract. I explain that this agreement will allow me to represent their interest rather than the seller's, but they are still so reluctant.

Suddenly, a light bulb went on in my head. When a colleague expressed her frustration about getting buyers to recognize that appointing a buyer agent helps them get the best deal, I saw things as homebuyers must see them. And heard the conversation that must go on in a buyer's head: something like…

> Who is this real estate agent in front of me? What are they anyway? Are they a salesperson trying to sell me a house, or are they some kind of consultant offering to represent my needs? If they are a salesperson, shouldn't they just be trying to sell me a property? What is all this talk about providing representation? And if they're a consultant I'm paying to represent my needs, then why is the amount of their compensation, or whether they get paid at all, wholly dependent on my decision or how much I spend?

This got me thinking. When I, as a consumer, deal with salespeople versus consultants, what are my expectations of each?

Suppose I want to buy a car. If I enter a showroom, I would expect someone to walk up and offer to help me. I would immediately identify that "someone" as a salesperson. My expectation would be that they would ask about my needs—the make of the car, model, color, features that I'm interested in. Then they should show me cars that might match those needs. I have a high regard for good salespeople, therefore, I would have the expectation that they would deal with me honestly and not misrepresent themselves, the dealership, or their vehicles. However, I would harbor no illusions that they were working for anyone other than their dealership and themselves.

But suppose that when I entered the showroom, someone came up and instead of showing me cars, whipped out a contract and said, "Before I start showing you around, I'd like you to consider signing this contract. By doing so, I can represent your interest rather than that of the dealership. And even though I'm paid by commission, signing this contract will allow me to negotiate the best deal on whatever car you decide to buy." If this happened, I would be really confused, and frankly, a bit skeptical.

This person wants to represent my needs and negotiate the best deal for me on a car, yet the amount of their compensation—or whether they get paid at all—is wholly dependent on my decision. And why would he will use his skills to negotiate the lowest price when he is paid a percentage?

That got me thinking about another scenario. Suppose I was having legal concerns regarding my finances. I would make an appointment to meet with a qualified attorney, and I'd expect to pay that attorney for a consultation either by an hourly fee or a flat rate. I would expect that she would use her expertise to advise me regarding my financial issues and assist me in a resolution. And because I was paying her for her time, expertise, and experience, I would most definitely have the expectation that her counsel would be completely objective.

Yet suppose during the consultation, the attorney started discussing some financial products that she sold on the side. "Instead of paying me by fee, you can buy one of these products. I'll get a commission on whatever I sell you and you'll end up paying less."

If this happened, not only would I be confused, I'd be out of there! I hired a professional to consult with me, not to sell to me. And I would be very skeptical about this attorney giving me truly objective advice if her pay was contingent on selling me something and on how much I spend overall.

Make no mistake, folks: The real estate industry is having an identity crisis because agents are being asked to fill two roles that are in conflict, especially in the mind of the consumer.

On one hand, real estate has always been considered a sales profession, paid by commission. As an independent contractor, a real estate agent needs to move the "inventory" as quickly as possible, and for as much money as possible, to make a living in this business.

And yet, if an agent is a Realtor® (most, but not all agents are, so make sure that the one you deal with is), he must follow a code of ethics which, among other things, requires him to put the needs and interests of his clients ahead of everyone else's, including and most especially, his own. While staying poised and performing in these two conflicting roles is an incredible balancing act, the overwhelming majority of my fellow agents walk that line everyday and they walk it well.

Despite what you might hear in the popular press (more on this later), most real estate agents are hard-working, honest, and ethical professionals who strive—sometimes at great financial sacrifice—to do right by their clients.

When working with a seller, most agents will recommend a listing price that will get the seller the most money in a reasonable period of time, even though underpricing it would make the home sell faster and assure the agent of being paid. Hence, the conflict of interest. Most listing agents will truthfully counsel a seller on what the market is doing. They may even suggest a seller not sell their home when the market doesn't favor a profitable sale, even though they only get paid if the seller does. When a seller has outgrown his home, I have known many an agent who has counseled him to remodel rather than move, even though they she just talked herself out of a job.

Now, let's look at the other side. When working with home buyers, buyer agents (who have a contractual obligation to work in their buyer's best interest) do every day what makes absolutely no sense on paper: Negotiate the lowest possible price for their buyer-clients even though they are paid as a percentage of that price.

That the vast majority of agents routinely put the needs and interests of their clients before their own is a testament to the industry and makes me very proud, but agents are doing so in spite of the commission system, not because of it.

One of the most common questions I have received from sellers over the years is "How do I know that you are pricing my, home for the best value rather than the speed of closing the sale?" And one of the most common questions from buyers is "Why would you negotiate the best deal for me when you get more money from a higher sale price?" I answer both the same way: "My business is built on referral. A few extra dollars in my pocket isn't going to mean beans when you find out that you sold for too little (sellers) or paid too much (buyers)." But while my answer is sound and reflects how I work, it still begs the questions of the inherent conflict of interest when you're compensated for moving product while charged with giving objective counsel.

"Please, Just Tell Me What I'm Paying For!"

In the same way that most agents are hard-working folks who strive to do right by their clients, the vast majority of consumers who are looking for alternatives appreciate what a good real estate professional brings to the table. They have no problem with paying for quality real estate assistance, if only they could make sense of what they are paying for.

If you're like most consumers, you probably have never really understood how the commission system works. In recent years, with housing prices so high, a 5, 6, or 7 percent commission can sometimes amount to more than the equity in your home. When the economy is good, home sellers may silently wonder about the commission system, but when the economy tightens, they increasingly become vocal and start asking agents some very logical questions:

1. "If I price my home where you tell me to, get it in tip-top condition, and make it easy to show, why am I paying the same thing as the guy down the street who does none of these things?"
2. "When my $600,000 home sells, I will be paying twice as much as my cousin across town who is selling a $300,000 home. Why is that? Do you do twice as much work? Or put in twice as much time?"

When agents complain to their brokers that it's getting more and more difficult to justify their commissions to the public, brokers overwhelmingly just tell them to show the client how much they do for them. And while I would agree that much of the public has no idea how much work is involved with selling a home, trotting out a list of the *450 Things That an Agent Does* misses the point.

As we'll see in a later chapter, paying by commission has nothing to do with compensating an agent for time or services. Commissions are all about mitigating risk. Until we, as an industry, are willing to provide choices, consumers will be increasingly left on their own without necessary services, expertise, or representation when selling their typically largest financial asset.

Let's face it, sometimes consumers have real estate needs that don't lend themselves to the traditional *full-marketing-package-payable-only-by-commission* setup. For example:

✦ Maybe the consumer happened to find an interested buyer on her own, but needs expert assistance in negotiating, trouble-shooting, and managing the transaction until it closes.

✦ Maybe a couple has outgrown their home (or their house has outgrown them) and they need objective counsel on whether to *move or improve.*

✦ Or, maybe a seller has no desire to play Realtor®, and needs a full package of services. He would like to pay the real estate professional for services rendered, the way he pays for most other service providers.

I believe it's high time that consumers are offered real choices in what services they want and how they would like to pay for them, as long as they understand these three basic economic realities:

1. It's a basic rule of Economics 101: high risk must equal high reward. If you, as a consumer, want the agent to take all the risk (i.e., you only want to pay an agent if you get your desired outcome), then you're going to have to pay a premium for that safety net.
2. On the other hand, if you would rather pay for an agent's services, expertise, and time rather than a convoluted percentage of your home's sale price, you can't have that compensation also be contingent on the sale. Just like any other service provider, if the agent provides the services and time, the agent needs to be paid for them.
3. If you only want to pay for a six-pack of beer, don't expect to receive a bottle of champagne. You get what you pay for. In

real estate, it's very easy to be enticed to go cheap—but while you'll save pennies, you'll drop dollars.

At the same time, I also believe that it's high time that hard-working agents stop working (and advertising their services) for free. Nothing in this world is free; not a market analysis advertised in the paper nor the "tour guide services" that agents routinely provide buyers. Unpaid hours of work need to be made up somewhere, and under the commission system, they are made up by the transactions that actually do close.

The Elephant in the Room

No matter how it's presented or dressed up, there is an inherent conflict of interest when a real estate professional is expected to act as a fiduciary agent providing objective, unbiased counsel to clients, while at the same time being paid by commission. This unspoken reality, combined with a lack of choices in the real estate services offered and how they can be paid for, is the elephant in the room. The real estate industry knows it's there because the consumer keeps pointing to it, but no one wants to acknowledge it and certainly no one wants to talk about it.

The industry has instead become expert at creating diversions, such as skimming a percentage point off the commission when the consumer complains, or charging an "administrative fee" to try to cover their costs, but these diversions are temporary and beg the answer to very real questions.

The industry nibbles at the corners because resolving the real issues requires a major paradigm shift in how the industry defines itself. It means a new way of thinking and acting, developing a whole new model in real estate. Dealing with the real issues means looking the consumer in the eye and telling the truth: Yes, commissions are high—they have to be! It's the price a consumer must pay for the agent and broker to take the risk.

The elephant is growing, and to continue to ignore its presence is to strip away your ability to get vital services and representation when buying or selling a home. You would be at the mercy of hucksters who would have you believe that selling a home is no more difficult than selling used clothes at a yard sale.

One of my favorite books is *Sacred Cows Make the Best Burgers* by Robert Kriegel and David Brandt. They explain why when tradition fails, it's time for change. I didn't write this book so bookstores would have another real estate how-to on their shelves. Frankly, there are enough real estate books on the shelves already and, sadly, most of them are either useless or downright misleading, written by people who have no clue about how real estate really works.

I wrote this book because it's time that we talk straight and clear and lay our cards on the table. It's time that the public is given a clear picture of what's really involved in buying or selling a house. Conversely, it's time for the real estate industry to start really listening to what the consumer is saying, and what you're asking for.

Agents need to stop selling and start consulting. The public deserves it and so does the hardworking agent.

PART ONE

The Current State of Real Estate

How in the World Did We Get Here

A Short History

THERE DOESN'T SEEM TO BE an exact date that real estate, as we know it, began. The practices of buying and selling property date back at least to the Old Testament, which documents real estate transactions by Abraham. The job of matching sellers and buyers of property for compensation has likely existed in some form since then.

What has become today's National Association of Realtors® was originally formed as a trade advocacy group in 1908, as the National Association of Real Estate Exchanges

Prior to 1908, licensing laws didn't exist; the real estate industry had a history of speculation and disorder. The new association did begin to regulate the practice of real estate. In 1913, this group, now known as the National Association of Real Estate Boards, adopted a Code of Ethics, with the Golden Rule as its theme.

While it states a goal of protecting the public interest, the primary focus of the Code of Ethics was to provide guidelines for arbitrating monetary disputes between Realtors®, as well as a basis for licensing laws. At this time real estate could not be defined as anything but a sales profession. While licensing laws began to protect the public from the most blatant exploitation, "buyer beware" was the rule. There was no representation or fiduciary responsibility as we know it.

In fact, until World War II, selling a home was no different than selling any other product. A broker had no fiduciary responsibilities. An agent could show a prospective buyer a home as a "tour guide," by demonstrating features and benefits. There were few, if any, disclosure requirements, as we know them now.

After World War II, the concept of agency, with the attendant protection and promotion of the interests of the client, became a more prominent consideration. This was the beginning of the dual role of the agent: first as a salesperson with a goal of selling properties, and second, as that of a fiduciary, protecting the client's interest .

From the 1940s through the 1980s, the focus was on sales. After all, the only clients were sellers and protecting their interests consisted primarily of getting them the most money for their property. There was little, if any, knowledge of environmental risks that must be disclosed, and, of course, the buyer had no representation. In addition, housing prices were much more in line with other necessities of life, so a 6 or 7 percent commission was rarely questioned.

In the mid-80s, the agent's role as a fiduciary began to grow. Knowledge and required disclosure of items, such as Urea-Formaldehyde Foam Insulation (UFFI), lead paint, and radon, began. While buyer representation was still largely unheard of, more and more states were requiring that agents and their brokers disclose that they were working in the interest of the seller.

Of course, the mid-80s brought a rapid increase in home prices (which later crashed) putting downward pressure on commissions, which now represented a far larger expense to the seller. The traditional sales model that had been in use for over 75 years was beginning to develop cracks. While there was little issue yet of conflicts of interest, sellers increasingly began questioning what they were paying for and why they paid so much in commission.

As buyer representation grew rapidly, a stagnant basic sales approach failed to accommodate the changing reality.

But the problems ran deeper. The consumer's perception of the agent as a salesperson paid by commission went hand-in-glove with a perception that the agent's value was as information gatekeeper. The emphasis on the role of salesperson rather than an advisor contributed to the public's belief that the agent was simply the *provider* of information rather than an *interpreter*.

The public focused on the agent as a functionary, rather than that of a fiduciary (more on this in a later chapter). As the Internet grew and access to information exploded, the Internet-savvy consumer increasingly believed that the real estate agent was replaceable. Today, in the era of eBay, craigslist.com, and almost universal access to the Multiple Listing Service (MLS), buyers already have access to the "inventory."

If that was the whole story, then there wouldn't be a need for this book. But, while do-it-yourself (DIY) can replace the agent's functionary services, the agent also plays a much more important role: as a *consultant* and an *advocate* whose value can never be replaced by technology. An agent's real value is in interpreting that raw data to the client's benefit.

Let's fast-forward to today. Because the public doesn't understand the true value of a real estate professional, buyers and sellers lose a great deal of time and money.

This is not the public's fault! Certainly the press has not helped with damning articles about real estate agents and their "salesperson" mentality, but the real culprit out there is the real estate industry itself. The business of real estate has changed incredibly over the last hundred years, but the sales model and practice have not.

There are many of us who think it's way past time that it did.

Both buyers and sellers will be better served when you can gain access to the huge expertise of a good agent, and compensate that agent fairly for her time, knowledge, and advice.

The Other Side of the Fence

GROWING UP, ONE OF THE SAYINGS I heard most was "Don't judge the next tribe until you've walked a mile in their moccasins." There are a lot of variations of this saying, yet the message is still very clear and important. I think it's human nature to make observations and sometimes to generalize about another group of people; this is often how we make sense of the world. Unfortunately, this practice leads to stereotypes, which have no connection to reality.

In talking with hundreds of consumers over the years, it's clear to me that many have misconceptions about how real estate works, how homes get bought and sold, and how easy (or not) it is for a real estate agent to make a living in this business. Fed by advertising ploys promising the world for a song and inaccurate articles about the industry masquerading as news, many consumers have developed a false impression about real estate. Without valid and complete information, they buy or sell a home through cheap discount companies or completely on their own, without advocacy or representation. And for the vast majority, this costs—rather than saves—your precious time and money.

At the same time, it's abundantly clear that the real estate industry has done an incredibly poor job of listening to the consumer. Instead of coming up with real options that give the consumer value for your dollar and flexibility in how you pay for real estate services, real estate companies either stubbornly stick to offering only the standard full-marketing package paid only by full commission, or they offer cut-rate commissions with shoddy services. These bare-bones services, without disclosing what they don't cover, often don't get the job done, thereby further eroding the value of the real estate professional in the consumer's mind.

Let's develop some understanding between the parties as we look at three typical real estate scenarios. While these consumers are fictional, and their experiences are a composite, both their good and bad experiences reflect today's new reality.

A Decision for Consumers

RICK AND SUE are in their early 30s with a 4-year-old son and a 1-year-old daughter. They have a decision to make. Rick was just offered a new job. The position sounds wonderful and the salary provides a nice raise. However, it's two hours away, so if he takes the job, they are going to have to move.

Rick and Sue really struggled to buy their present house four years ago. Then it was a "seller's market" with sky-high prices and five buyers for every available home. But Rick and Sue had also learned a valuable lesson—unfortunately from the disastrous experience of many of their friends—and so they hired a buyer's agent to help them buy this present home.

Many of Rick and Sue's friends had "gone it alone" in buying a home. It seemed at the time that all the media could talk about was all the online home listings. Rick and Sue learned a particularly valuable lesson from their friends Bob and Liz.

BOB AND LIZ bought a home a year before Rick and Sue did. They both worked in the high-tech field so they were able to take advantage of the "wealth" of free online real estate information and services. They signed up on several agent property searches, and when they saw a home that looked interesting, they would drive by the house and call the agent on the sign. Of course, there were several things that Bob and Liz didn't understand. First that even though the property searches were free to them, they certainly weren't free to the agents who provided them, and in fairness, these agents should have been given the opportunity to show them homes of interest. But like a majority of the population, Bob and Liz didn't think about this, simply because they didn't know. And Bob and Liz figured that the agent on the sign was the best person to call—after all, they would know the most about this particular house, right?

Wow, did Bob and Liz get burned! They put in an offer on one of the homes with the listing agent on the sign. The agent was nice enough, but told them that there was already another offer on the house, so they'd better put in an overbid if they wanted it. As the current list price of the house was $372,000, they had to pay $15,000 over the list price—$387,000—in order to get the house. They found out later that the agent was pitting one buyer against the other, trying to get the highest price for their seller. The agent didn't do anything wrong— after all, the seller was his client and the agent's job was to work in his client's best interest.

But worse for Bob and Liz, they asked the listing agent for a recommendation on a home inspector. At the time, Bob and Liz figured that they probably should check out other inspectors, but they were under so much pressure! The agent kept telling them that they better not ask for anything else because there were two other back-up offers.

After they closed on the house, they found out that the inspector missed a leak in the roof. He also failed to tell them that much of the exterior siding had rotted as well as the underlying boards from pest infestation. Bob and Liz ended up having to replace the roof and much of the siding at a cost of over $30,000. They now had $417,000 invested in their home.

Last month, they decided to refinance and were devastated to discover that they had no equity. Not only did they overpay for the house and put another $30,000 into it for repairs, but the market had shifted and prices were dropping. It would be years before they could financially recover from this purchase. Regardless, they had an agent do a market analysis (after all, agents are always advertising them as free), but they found out that if they were going to sell today, they would probably lose over $50,000.

This story gave Rick and Sue nightmares as they considered their options.

KATIE AND MIKE. Another couple that Rick and Sue were friendly with, Katie and Mike, got screwed on their mortgage. They went with a company that Mike found online that promised "unbelievable" rates. Because they were buying direct from a For-Sale-By-Owner (or FSBO, pronounced phiz-bow, for short) there was no one to caution them about the risks of getting a mortgage online. The mortgage field is very competitive, and online lenders often get their business from advertising, not word-of-mouth, so they can offer false promises regarding rates and programs without being held accountable.

Katie and Mike chose an online lender whose rates were too good to pass up and, as things happen, the problems started soon after they signed the purchase and sale agreement. They were concerned when they heard from the seller that no appraiser had called to schedule an appraisal of the property. Katie and Mike emailed the lender several times, trying to find out if the appraisal had been ordered. They were told that if the appraisal wasn't done in a timely fashion, they might not get their loan commitment by the due date. This was very serious. They risked losing their entire deposit, which in their case was 20 percent, or $77,000.

Sure enough, when the lender finally got in touch with them, he said that he was sorry, things got backed up, but he would get someone out there right away. On the day before the commitment date, the lender called Mike and Katie to tell them that he couldn't get them the promised program after all, but that they were really "lucky" because he was able to find another investor. This loan carried a much higher interest rate; higher, in fact, than the rate offered by the local lenders that had been originally recommended to them. Katie and Mike were completely frustrated, but what could they do? It was too late to bring in another lender because if they didn't make the commitment date, the sellers would be able to keep the entire deposit.

So Katie and Mike had to accept the loan with an interest rate that was a full two points higher than what they could have gotten with a local lender. Worse, the online lender didn't even return their calls when they complained. But why should that lender somewhere out there in "dot-com-land" even care? Unlike a local lender who gets their business from referrals and real estate agents, and hopefully aims to be a respected member of the community, online lenders get theirs primarily from advertising. If someone gets a bad deal it doesn't hurt their reputation; they just go on to the next borrower.

Back to Rick and Sue. They had hired Marlene Brady, a buyer agent who had come recommended, to assist them in buying their first home two years ago. Marlene was great and helped them to avoid the disasters that befell their friends. Because she was working in Rick and Sue's interest, her recommended home inspector was not only efficient but also thorough. In fact, when he inspected the first house they put an offer on, it turned out to have major structural problems and Marlene was able to get their deposit back. The second home they put an offer on, they bought, and it happened to be a much better house and a much better deal.

As good as Marlene was however, she couldn't help them too much on the price—housing prices were still high. Rick and Sue felt that if they waited for prices to stabilize, interest rates would have risen, negating any savings. Besides, Marlene told them that usually, as long as they stayed in the house at least five years, the market would have time to recover.

Now, only four years later, Rick and Sue faced a decision. Marlene had stayed in touch with them so there was no question of who they would call to sell their home. But when she came over, she had bad news. The market had changed from a seller's market four years earlier to a buyer's market now. Market time was increasing and prices were plummeting. After doing a market analysis, Marlene told them honestly that the best they could hope for was to break even if they wanted to sell now. Of course, that was before commissions and when they did some calculations, they realized that even a 5 percent commission (which was lower than the going rate) was more than the equity they had accrued.

They were honest with Marlene. They told her that they wanted to hire her, but they just couldn't afford a full commission. They asked her if there were any other options. Marlene explained that commissions were the way agents were paid and the only way to save money was to discount the commission. Yet even if she was willing to cut her commission, her company wouldn't allow it—after all, under the commission system, the company was taking all the risk, and if the house didn't sell, Rick and Sue wouldn't owe any money. Marlene explained that discounting commissions doesn't work well in a slow market. When commissions are cut, they are cut not just on the listing side, but also to the buyer's agent. And with plenty of houses to choose from, their home would be at a disadvantage.

Rick and Sue considered if there were other options they might have to save some money. They definitely did not want to try to sell their own house. They knew six people who'd tried to and only one was successful. With both of them working full time, when would they be able to show their home?

Besides, they found out that Jay, their one friend who was successful in selling his own home, wasn't so successful after all. Jay told them that playing Realtor® wasn't as easy as all the For-Sale-By-Owner websites said it was. After weeks of holding open houses every Sunday, all he had to show for it was $1000 dollars lost to advertising, with no offers. Finally a buyer came along with an offer, but it was really low. It was clear that the buyer had deducted the same commission that he was trying to save and then some. Jay knew that he was being taken advantage of, but after five months on the market, he was tired of being tied to the house and felt that he had been misled by all those "do-it-yourself" websites. When all was said and done, he sold his own house, but ended up getting 15 percent less than what comparable homes were selling for. He could have paid even an 8 percent commission and still come out way ahead! Jay told Rick and Sue that if he had it to do over again, he would definitely hire a professional agent.

Sue was also concerned about the lack of security in showing strangers their home. If they listed their house with Marlene, they could be assured that people looking at their home were real buyers; people who had qualified financially. But without an agent, how would Rick and Sue know if these people were real buyers or Jack the Ripper? With two small children, Sue was not going to take that risk.

Then one day Rick heard on the radio about a company that provided "limited service." For $500 they could pay an agent to put their listing in the Multiple Listing Service (MLS) and all they had to do was to pay the agent who brought the buyer! Rick and Sue trusted Marlene and really wanted to be able to pay her for all of her good advice, so they immediately called her and asked if her company could do the same thing.

Another disappointment. Marlene told them that this "MLS Entry Only" idea was a really poor one. She explained that the MLS was never intended to be used in this way and her experience was that even if a seller offered a competitive commission to the agent bringing the buyer and no listing agent, most agents wouldn't show these homes. With plenty of other homes on the market, most agents didn't want to have to deal directly with the seller and do double work. Marlene further explained that all they were buying for their $500 was twenty minutes of typing. Rick and Sue would be on their own, with no one to advise them or to help them with negotiating offers and guiding the transaction to close. She told them that her company would not participate in what was clearly a terrible deal for the sellers who tried it.

By this time, Rick and Sue were totally frustrated. They appreciated what a quality agent like Marlene brought to the table, and knew they needed and wanted professional help. But there seemed no way to get that help for a cost they could afford. They even asked Marlene if they could try to find a buyer on their own and pay her by the hour to negotiate for them. Marlene told them no, unfortunately her company was traditional and commissions were the only method of payment. While she personally would be happy to be paid in another way, her brokerage would not allow it.

Rick declined the new position offered to him. He and Sue instead decided to work hard and batten down the hatches for a few more years.

I'm Paying You How Much?

Why Commissions Are so High

WHY ARE COMMISSIONS SO HIGH? This is the constant question that we in the industry hear from consumers, more than any other question or concern. Most consumers who ask it will tell you that it's not that they don't want to pay a reasonable amount for quality real estate services, they just want to understand what it is that they're paying for. If you have also asked this question, then I think it's time that you got a straight answer.

When you pay a real estate commission on a closed transaction, you are not simply paying for the services rendered to you on that one single transaction. If you were paying for the services themselves, you would be paying a lot less.

When you pay for real estate services by commission, the lion's share of what you are paying for is not the services themselves, but rather paying for "insurance."

In other words, you are paying a premium for a guaranteed outcome, an assurance that if you don't achieve the desired outcome, you pay nothing.

Therefore, you, as the consumer, pay a premium but have no risk. The agent assumes a high risk but a high reward if successful. That's how the traditional real estate system works.

An Example: The Personal Injury Attorney

The commission system in real estate is very similar to an attorney being paid on contingency. Most people understand that when attorneys take high-risk personal injury cases, for example, there's a good chance that they could put in many hours of work and never see a dime. Their services are "free" to their client until they win the case. But if they are successful, their reward is high—personal injury attorneys usually collect at least a third of the award.

Now suppose this attorney is successful on a particular case. If you are to just look at that one case, her "pay" would seem like an incredible amount of money for the time invested. But that large paycheck has to compensate the attorney not just for the hours put in on that one particular case, but for all the many unpaid hours on the cases that were lost. In fact, if you took a personal injury attorney's gross income for a year and divided it by the total number of hours worked on all cases that year, her pay per hour would probably seem very reasonable for the expertise, knowledge, and experience.

Suppose that a client complained about the large amount their attorney would receive if they were successful in litigating their case. Suppose they were to ask their attorney to take the same high-risk case but to take less of a percentage? How would the attorney respond? If she was either not very good at her job, or rather desperate for business, she might take the bait and cut her contingent compensation. At the same time, she would probably cut her quality of the work and reduce time invested in that case, greatly diminishing the chances for success. Why? Because it is still high risk but now low reward. Who wants that?

In this situation, most attorneys with a reputation for quality work would tell the consumer that if the attorney takes all the risk, the attorney must receive a high reward. Otherwise, from a pure dollars-and-cents perspective, this method of compensation is unbalanced and doesn't work.

Like the attorney being paid on a contingency, under the commission system in real estate, an agent's compensation is dependent on a favorable outcome—an outcome he can influence but not control.

The difference in the comparison however, between a real estate agent and a personal injury attorney, is that while most consumers understand the inherent risks in a personal injury case, most are not aware of the risks inherent in the daily work of an agent assisting buyers and sellers. Unless they or someone close to them have worked in the field, most people don't recognize the countless hours that agents typically put in, but are never paid for. Many consumers are under the impression that most real estate transactions close. But nothing could be farther from the truth! To further illustrate this point, let's look at a few more case studies—this time from the agent's point of view:

✦ Sandy and Scott Seller are ready to sell their home. Sandy's Aunt Doris is a part-time agent who lives out of the area. Sandy would like to give their listing to Aunt Doris, except that Auntie doesn't know the local market and therefore doesn't know how to price their home. But Scott doesn't see it as a problem at all. After all, every time he opens the local paper, there are at least three or four agents that are advertising a "free" comparative market analysis (CMA). So he calls three of them, tells each of them he's going to be selling his home, and he would like them to prepare a CMA for him. Now, while those CMAs are free to Scott and Sandy, to the agents, there is nothing free about them. A high-quality CMA takes approximately four hours to prepare, not to mention the time spent presenting them in hopes of getting the listing. In this case, none of the agents are going to get the listing. When Aunt Doris lists the house, those three agents will discover that they've just put in a lot of work that they'll never be paid for.

✦ Bob and Barbara Buyer are looking to buy their first home. They interview several agents and decide that they like Betty Buyer Agent the best. Betty smartly requires that they sign an exclusive buyer agency contract with her. She's been burned in the past by working weeks or months with buyers only to have them call on an ad and buy with someone else. This way she's protected, right? Not so fast! After months of working with Bob and Barbara, Bob gets a new job out of state. The local house search is off and even though Betty has spent many hours with Bob and Barbara, she'll never get paid.

✦ Sam Seller has been reading that the market is very slow. This concerns him since he would like to sell his house and retire but only if he can "get his price." But even though the market is soft, Sam figures that it doesn't cost him anything to try—he knows that he only has to pay if the agent is successful. He tells several agents that he'd like to sell his home but only if he can get a price of $$ (about 20% over the current market price). Most agents smartly turn him down, but a couple of agents really need the business and hope that if they take his listing, they can convince him to moderate his price later. Andrea Agent "wins" the listing and goes to work. She expends a lot of money on materials and advertising and countless hours marketing the home. Sadly, Sam can't afford to sell unless he can get his unrealistic price so after six weeks, he decides to pull his house off the market and wait for better times. Andrea Agent's wasted time and money are not his concern.

I'm not citing these examples to make you feel sorry for real estate agents, but to show you that the common perception that under the commission system real estate agents are all driving Bentleys and vacationing in the Caribbean is just a dangerous myth. In fact, our research at the Accredited Consultant in Real Estate (ACRE®) shows the sad truth: with all the requirements, training, liability, and continuing education, the average agent today earns less than minimum wage.

Most agents are shocked at how little they actually make per hour. It's because they don't think in terms of hourly worth. When we as agents get a check, we almost always forget how many unpaid hours (and transactions that fell apart) that check has to cover before we can move forward toward profit (and our Bentleys and Caribbean vacations).

Please note that in each of the previous examples, the consumer did nothing wrong. Sandy, Scott, and Sam were simply taking advantage of some "free" services. And it's certainly no fault of Bob and Barbara that they've been transferred. My point is that all those unpaid hours and accrued expenses have to be made up somewhere. And they're made up by the transactions that do successfully close.

Of course, if you're like many home sellers I speak with, you may feel it's not fair to "subsidize" the consumers that use agents' time and resources but don't ever buy or sell. I agree with you, it's not fair; and with housing prices at an all time high and consumer debt rising so fast over the last few years, a 5, 6, or 7 percent commission can and will often be a prohibitive cost. For both the agent and the consumer, this situation is lose-lose.

When I speak with a seller who complains that commissions are high, I do feel for them, but I am also compelled to tell them the truth. As Blanche Evans, editor of Realty Times explained in an article:

> What agents need to explain to their customers and clients is that with commissions, they're paying for risk mitigation. The reason they pay a commission is to offload some or most of the risk onto the real estate agent. Those risks include making sure the paperwork...will stand up in a dispute, protecting the home from being entered by unqualified buyers who may be more interested in raiding the medicine cabinet than buying a home, and making sure all the steps to closing are met on time and with professionalism by all parties....
>
> An important part of risk is money. If the client were to go to the bank and ask for an unsecured loan to pay for marketing their home, what would be the bank charge? Pull out a credit card. Most credit cards charge 18 percent and higher. And those are loans that have to be paid back or the bank can ruin the cardholder's credit. If an agent doesn't sell a house, they have to absorb the marketing costs and the seller pays nothing. So, is charging 6% when you have to share the money with another agent and the transaction may not close, too high?

You would think that we could put our heads together—real estate practitioners and consumers alike—and come up with some alternative types of compensation for those consumers who would like quality and full service, but who neither want, nor want to pay, a premium for the "insurance policy" that paying-by-commission provides. And wouldn't it be nice, for example, if consumers could pay a flat fee for a thorough, objective CMA if that's all they need? Or perhaps the consumer could hire a real estate professional by the hour to consult with about his real estate needs. The consumer would be confident that the advice would be truly objective, because the agent is being paid for her time and expertise.

Instead of coming up with some alternative methods of compensation, many in the real estate industry have responded by cutting the amount and quality of services offered in exchange for a discount commission. Unfortunately, the services that often get cut are the very ones that make all the difference in the bottom line of a buying or selling transaction.

There is an alternative, and that is paying for the vital fiduciary services that make consumers money without paying for the fluff that doesn't generate a profit. How to tell the difference? It lies in understanding the crucial difference between functionary tasks and fiduciary counsel. Knowing where to put your money can save you thousands! To learn more, let's take a look at the next chapter, *What an Agent Does: Functionary Tasks Versus Fiduciary Counsel.*

FROM THE CONSULTING TIMES:

Living a Double Business Life—
A Tale of Two Seafood Shops

By ACRE® Mollie Wasserman

IN THE ARTICLE, "Discount Brokerages Band Together" Matt Carter of Inman News wrote that Virginia-based RebateReps.com helps agents who want to dabble in discounting without alienating full-commission customers, or work for a discount broker full time. "Most Realtors® don't want to advertise themselves as rebate agents because it cannibalizes their other business," said RebateReps founder and owner Daniel Rubén Odio-Páez. "RebateReps connects buyers to local agents who are willing to rebate part of their commission but don't necessarily want to advertise that fact." Odio-Páez said. "RebateReps allows agents to have their full-service brokerage and to service our (discount commission) leads."

I find it fascinating that these discount and rebate firms can find agents willing to cut their contingent commissions (while continuing to take all the risk, I might add), as long as they can "do it on the sly." But I'm wondering how long these agents can keep their double life going. What happens when their "full paying" clients find out about the rebates they are handing out to others? Sounds like a two-tiered system: give rebates or cut your commissions to only those consumers who demand it, while continuing to charge whatever you can to consumers who are too "unenlightened" to ask for a break.

Folks, this is what a broken compensation system, out of step with the realities of today's real estate landscape, has wrought.

I'd like to tell you a tale of two seafood shops. Shop "A" displays only its expensive and most profitable seafood, like shrimp and lobster. They do carry more moderately priced fish like flounder or sole, but since they don't make quite as much money on these, they would rather not display them, thinking that if the customer doesn't see the less expensive fish, they'll simply buy what's displayed.

Of course, every once in awhile, a customer will come up and ask the owner if they carry flounder or sole. The owner will quickly glance around to make sure no one else is looking, and then bring out the less expensive fish from behind the counter, but the owner's policy is to keep the flounder and sole stashed away, out of sight, and, he reasons, out of the customer's mind.

Now, note that Shop "A" still makes a very tidy profit when selling the less expensive fish, but just not as much as from the shrimp and lobster. But, there's one little problem with the owner's reasoning. Every day, many potential customers walk by his shop, look in the window and, only seeing shrimp and lobster when they wanted to buy flounder and sole, just keep on walking to Shop "B."

Shop "B" has a very different philosophy: the store displays all the seafood that it carries, pricing each type of seafood as competitively as possible while still earning a reasonable profit. If shrimp and lobster cost them more at the dock, they charge more, but they let the customer choose what seafood they want. What is interesting is that customers who come in thinking that they want flounder or sole often "trade up" to shrimp and lobster because when they are able to compare the options side by side, they can see that while the shrimp and lobster cost more, it's worth it.

At the same time, the shop almost never sees a shrimp or lobster customer downgrade to less expensive fish. On the contrary, upon seeing other choices, they become more content in their choice.

Today's Internet-savvy consumer, who has unprecedented access to data, is looking for two major things from a real estate professional—and will get neither from the double-life agents who offer discounts and rebates on the sly:

✦ **CHOICES** in the services they can receive and how they can pay for them. If someone wants shrimp and lobster, they are not going to buy flounder just because it's offered side by side with more expensive seafood. But they will feel that they made the BEST choice, not the ONLY one. When given a choice in real estate, many consumers will choose a full-service package and often, will be more comfortable paying by commission. But, they will not try to beat down the agent on that commission because they understand that the "insurance policy" is why commissions have to be high compared to paying for the services themselves.

✦ What my ACRE® colleague Merv Forney calls **TRANSPARENCY**. More than cost savings, today's consumers simply want to understand what real estate services they are paying for. When a real estate professional explains that commissions are higher than fees because the risk is borne by the agent, they understand and can make informed choices, just as they do when they see a well-stocked display of seafood. What customers are saying loud and clear today is that they don't like it when the options are "hidden behind the counter."

Instead of offering rebates and discounts on the sly, why not price our services competitively and let the consumer choose between paying for the services and/or time itself or by commission, which provides the services with insurance? Some consumers will choose to pay for the services themselves, and if the practitioner has priced their services to earn a reasonable profit, then the practitioner should be happy too.

And many consumers, once understanding that commissions pay for risk mitigation in addition to services, will continue to choose commissions. They just want choices and transparency—not double-life agents.

What an Agent Does

Functionary Tasks Versus Fiduciary Counsel

IN REAL ESTATE, KNOWING WHERE TO PUT YOUR MONEY can save you thousands. That's because real estate agents are not commodities, as I elaborate on in the next chapter. Different agents provide different levels and different quality of service.

Almost anyone can go into real estate. You don't need a bachelor's degree; you don't even need a two-year associate's degree. Just for comparison, in my home state of Massachusetts, you must complete 100 classroom hours if you want to be licensed as a manicurist. If you want to be licensed as a cosmetologist, it's 1000 classroom hours. But if you want to be licensed to guide consumers through the largest and perhaps the most emotional financial purchase or sale of their lives, you need only complete 24 hours of classroom training. Twenty-four! A day's worth!

Here is a joke that one of my colleagues from California told me:

> I have a friend who was pulled over yesterday for speeding. The police officer asked him for his registration and real estate license. "Don't you mean my driver's license?" he asked. "No," said the officer, "I mean your real estate license. Not everyone has a driver's license."

But being good enough to stay in real estate is another matter entirely. "The turnover of new agents is tremendous," says Paul Gorney, director of agent selection at Agents Across America, an online network of real estate agents. He estimates that seven out of ten new agents will leave real estate within two years.

And according to RealtyU® Group, the largest career development company and network of real estate schools in the country, approximately 50 percent of all new licensees leave the industry before their first anniversary.

To last in real estate and to have a productive business over the long haul, an agent must not only have the marketing, sales, and organizational skills to perform the functionary tasks needed for the job, but more importantly, the expertise, knowledge, and experience to provide the fiduciary counsel that will make all the difference in their clients' bottom line.

If you want to get your best value when you sell a home, it's vital to understand the difference between functionary tasks and fiduciary counsel.

Functionary Tasks

Functionary tasks are what most sellers think of when they are asked what a listing agent does. They include installing a lock box, taking digital photos of the exterior and interiors of the home, producing feature sheets that showcase its amenities, and installing a yard sign. These functionary tasks are important and need to be done to successfully sell a home for top dollar. Here's the catch: while they often are done more easily by a real estate professional, many of these tasks can be done by an assistant, or even by the homeowner. For a homeowner with the right skills and enough time, doing your own functionary tasks can save money. Thus, functionary tasks should not be the reason to hire a listing agent.

> *A good listing agent's highest value is not in locating buyers, though that's certainly important. A listing agent's highest value lies in negotiating the best deal, and then troubleshooting the transaction for their seller client once the buyer is found.*

Likewise, if you were to ask most home buyers what a buyer agent does for them, they would list things like doing home searches, making appointments, or running paperwork around. Again, these are functionary tasks, and while important, they can often be delegated. Certainly, buyers can save themselves a lot of time by first doing "drive-bys" of homes for sale, to learn neighborhoods and towns. But playing "tour guide" should not be the reason one hires a buyer's agent.

> *A good buyer agent's highest value is not in finding a home, though she certainly has the technology tools to do so. Her highest value is in getting the best deal for her buyer-client once the home is found.*

Here's a news flash: some functionary tasks, such as staffing a public open house (except in a rampant seller's market) are pure frill and are often only performed by agents as a way to justify their commission. Later in this chapter, I will discuss why open houses are a needless, and possibly perilous, functionary task.

Fiduciary Counsel

Fiduciary Counsel, on the other hand, does require the expertise, knowledge, and experience that a quality real estate professional brings to the table. This is what he does every day. It's the market knowledge, judgment of price and value, and thorough, ethical representation. It's not just the gathering of data, but the interpreting of that data. Some examples of fiduciary counsel on the listing side are...

+ Determining price and positioning of a home in the current local market
+ Sensing and communicating with the seller when the market is changing
+ Negotiating offers for the best price and terms
+ Troubleshooting the transaction to close, so it doesn't "flip," forcing the seller to start all over again.

It is the fiduciary counsel that the cut-rate real estate companies scrimp on—and that's when the consumer gets burned. The importance of fiduciary counsel is often overlooked by sellers going it alone (or with minimal help from a cheap firm) And in their zest to save money, these sellers end up losing far more. Sellers may shave a percentage point from a real estate commission, but the lack of professional counsel will net the seller thousands less. A seller going it alone will most likely misread the market, negotiate poorly on her own behalf (an exceedingly difficult task), pay her attorney double for tasks that an agent could have done better (because it's what we do), or fail to steer around the potholes that often come up between an accepted offer and a close.

If you're going to spend money on professional real estate assistance, put your money in the areas of fiduciary counsel. It will pay you back countless times over.

FUNCTIONARY TASKS	FIDUCIARY COUNSEL
Low Level	High Level
Delivers Information and Directions	Advises and Consults
Does the Task	Owns the Result
Responds to Needs and Processes Data	Anticipates Needs and Interprets Data
Shows the House	Determines the Value
Low Skill	High Skill
Follows Rules and Procedures	Uses Expert Judgment and Intuition
Valuable but Replaceable	Irreplaceable

* Adapted from Keller Williams' Realty Fiduciary

But All I Want Is a Big Burger!

Imagine you live in a world where all fast food outlets worked like the real estate industry. In this world when you drive up to the billboard menu to order, the conversation would go like this:

Billboard Voice: Welcome to Hungry Harry's! What value meal would you like today?

You: I don't want a whole meal, I just want a big burger.

Billboard Voice: We don't sell big burgers by themselves. We sell them as a part of a value meal: big burger, supersize fries, extra-large drink, and apple pie. That's the way we sell our food.

You: But I'm not that hungry and I don't want to pay that much.

Billboard Voice: Our policy is to only sell food as a meal. But, I'll tell you what—you can order our discount value

	meal, and we'll take two dollars off, and eliminate the big burger since you said you're not that hungry.
You:	But the big burger is what I really want.
Billboard Voice:	I'm sorry, but we don't do it that way. And you really need to make up your mind. You're holding up the line and since we're selling so many of these discount meals, we need to take as many orders as we can. We're only allowed to give two minutes to people wanting the discount meal.
	You start to think that maybe you should just go home and make your own hamburger. But your cooking skills are lousy, you don't have the time, and meanwhile you're really hungry. At least the fries and apple pie will fill your belly.
You:	OK, I guess I'll take the discount meal.

I figure by now you're seeing the parallel. Traditionally, the real estate industry has sold their services in bundles only, and when pressured by the consumer to have other options, some brokers and agents have responded by cutting their commissions and at the same time, cutting out services. Sadly, like the above example, it's the important item (the burger) that often gets cut rather than the empty calories (fries and apple pie).

My thanks to colleague Heather Jones Taylor for the fast food analogy. The fast food chain cited above is fictional and any resemblance to an actual fast food chain is strictly coincidence.

The Truth About Public Open Houses

You want to hear one of the best kept secrets in real estate? Public open houses are rarely ever instrumental in selling a house.

In the article, "Is an Open House a Waste of Time?" on MSN's website, Los Angeles real estate agent Liz Johnson, states that she loves open houses, but not because they move her properties. The real reason Johnson holds them is because they bring her more business. Prospective home buyers walk through and ask what other listings she has. "They've always been better for agents than sellers," she writes. Johnson is not alone. It's common knowledge among real estate agents that open houses are not very effective in actually selling a house.

That doesn't mean that sales don't happen at public open houses. It's just that it is likely that the sale would have occurred anyway. Most serious, qualified buyers today have their own agent. With buyer agency rapidly becoming the standard in many parts of the country, as time moves on, there will be fewer and fewer serious buyers that won't have their own agent. Represented buyers can have their agent schedule a home viewing anytime, so they don't have to wait for a public open house to see it. And sellers have the peace of mind knowing that any buyers who enter their home have been qualified by an agent and are in fact buyers.

The truth is, public open houses usually attract one of two types of people: would-be buyers who are just starting the process and not ready or not qualified to buy, or nosy neighbors who'd like to see how you decorated your home. Seriously! My mom (though she is certainly not nosy, just interested in the design and features of homes) loves open houses! If she has a Sunday afternoon available and there are interesting homes being held "open," she likes being able to see different home features while staying anonymous. I can guarantee you that she is not a buyer, but is simply someone taking advantage of a practice that has outlived its usefulness.

And why don't most agents tell the consumer the truth about public open houses?

- ✦ Most sellers expect open houses since they believe that they actually sell the homes.

- ✦ If an agent doesn't have good marketing skills, original and effective techniques for bringing listings to the attention of likely buyers and their agents, and/or the technology skills to showcase their listings online, open houses show the seller that they are at least doing something to earn their commission.

- ✦ They are an avenue of new business for the agent. Those brand new buyers will almost never buy the house that is being held open, but sometimes they can become new customers for other homes.

The biggest reason that agents don't tell the public the truth about open houses is that it's much easier to keep holding open houses every Sunday than to tell the seller what they may not want to hear, especially in a slow market. Most homes will sell for the right price, but no number of open houses are going to sell an overpriced home. Ever.

An Opening for Crime

But hey, if agents are OK with spending every Sunday sitting at someone's house, and sellers are OK with vacating their house every Sunday, I wouldn't be as tempted to blow the cover on this outdated practice. I feel compelled to speak the truth because in today's world not everyone looking at houses are legitimate buyers or even harmless "lookie-loos" like my mom. Some "visitors" have no interest in the house itself. Their interest lies in its contents and sometimes the person (either an agent or the seller themselves) who is showing it, often alone.

Sadly, over the last decade, there have been increasing incidents nationwide of theft and/or violence against an agent or homeowner who is by herself and showing a home—most especially at a public open house:

✦ In August of 2004, Colorado agent Garland Taylor was slain during a showing of a $900,000 listing by a well-groomed and professionally dressed man who is believed to have called Taylor from a pay phone and arranged to see the luxury property.

✦ In November of 2005, in Ventura, California, homeowner Larry Givens was robbed during an open house by a "buyer" who came in at the same time as a group of others and stole jewelry that had been put away in a drawer while Givens was distracted showing his home to other visitors.

✦ In July of 2006, agent Sarah Ann Walker in McKinney, Texas, was presiding over an open house at a new housing development when she was stabbed 27 times.

Certainly crime can occur at a scheduled showing as well as at an open house. The difference is that if someone calls to schedule an appointment, the agent has the time and resources to qualify them, as well as to determine whether the visitor is, in fact, a buyer. But a public open house is "public." Anyone can walk in and the agent has neither the time nor the tools to verify the visitor's intentions. Think about the following scenario:

A well-dressed and friendly stranger rings the bell at an open house. As the agent shows her around, she seems taken with the home and asks to take some digital photos so her husband, who is away on business, can see the pictures online. The agent is excited that perhaps she has an interested buyer for her listing. In fact, the prospective buyer has just taken pictures of some of the seller's most valuable possessions and documented the location of the rooms. If the seller has a home security system, she may have taken a picture of the motion detectors and the security key pad in preparation for another, less well-intentioned visit.

If public open houses were a sure-fire way of selling homes, I would continue to ask homeowners to put everything of value away, take the proper safety precautions, and hope for the best. But given the poor performance of an open house in actually selling the property, is holding your home "open" worth the risk?

That is why, if a seller insisted on an open house despite our warnings, my team would only hold the home open as a team—two of us can better keep an eye on the visitors as well as each other. If you still believe that holding your home open to strangers is worth the risk, please be safe. Put away your valuables and if you are unrepresented by an agent and holding the open house yourself, don't do it alone.

Consumers often don't understand why commissions are so high, and many have responded by seeking out discount real estate companies or agents. As we will see in the next chapter, accepting a flawed commission system and simply reducing the compensation is no bargain. Rather than cutting useless functionary tasks, these discount agencies will simply claim to give you "full service for less." But nothing comes free. Overwhelmingly, the fiduciary duties, counsel, and care get shortchanged when you pay a discount commission. These are the very things that return the most value for your real estate dollar when you hire a professional.

Here's an example from another industry entirely: my colleague Judi Bryan tells the story of her frugal daughter Shannon, a runner. She finally broke down and bought a new pair of running shoes shortly before a big race—but she bought on price, not quality. When the big day came, Shannon had to drop out of the race with horrible foot pain and nurse her abused feet back to health over time. The low-price offering proved to be low value, as well, and she was lucky she didn't permanently injure her feet. Similarly, when you use the lowest-priced broker, you may have to slowly nurse your injured financial status back to health over time.

Why a Discount Commission Is No Bargain

AS SMART CONSUMERS, one of the first things we learn to do is determine whether a product or service is:

+ **a commodity**, which can and should be shopped by price OR
+ a service, where the quality, level of expertise, talent, or experience of the practitioner can make a big difference in the outcome.

Let's look at an example of both:

My two sons wear "Brand X" socks. I find that "Brand X" fits the best and lasts the longest, so I stick to that brand. "Brand X" is sold in a package of three pairs and is available at a variety of outlets. Whether I buy this package of "Brand X" socks at the fanciest department store or at the cheapest discounter, the package of socks is the same. It's a commodity and, therefore, being a smart consumer, I shop it by price.

Let's contrast that with this scenario:

Suppose you just found out you won the lottery. After you finished your initial celebration and polished off some champagne, my guess is that the next day you would go out and hire yourself the best tax attorney you could get your hands on. And you would know that he was the best because he wouldn't come cheap. But, you'd gladly pay his hefty fee because you would know that whatever he charged would be greatly eclipsed by what he would save you. That's because tax attorneys are not commodities. Their expertise and experience make an enormous difference in how much of your lottery winnings go to the government and how much will stay in your pocket.

Expertise and experience are the key factors when judging most service professionals. For instance, many of us have learned the hard way that when we need our house painted, it's worth the extra money to hire a painter who is known for their quality work. This is because a cheap painter isn't so cheap when you have to have the job done over. And what about using a cheap plumber who takes shortcuts that flood your bathroom? Once you've had that happen, I guarantee you'll go with an experienced plumber next time, even if she costs more. Most of us learn fairly quickly that hiring cheap service providers is what my mom calls, "penny wise and pound foolish."

Hiring a quality painter or plumber is wise; choosing a qualified professional to handle more important concerns, like your finances and your health, is imperative. An experienced and skilled financial planner will make you money, whereas a bad one will just cost you money. Do you want the cheapest attorney if you're in legal trouble, or the cheapest dentist doing your root canal? If your child is ill, do you want to go to a pediatrician fresh out of medical school or a more seasoned practitioner, even if it costs you more?

You might say to the previous examples: "Of course, I would hire a quality person; these are important issues to me." Yet, often when the public looks for a mortgage lender or a real estate agent—someone to guide them in purchasing or selling their largest financial asset—the outlook often gets cloudy. Why? Because much of these professionals' value is behind the scenes, or maybe because they are usually compensated by commissions. Regardless, many consumers mistakenly believe that lenders and agents are a commodity and, therefore, shop them by price. But are they? Let's take a closer look.

First, let's look at mortgage lenders and online, do-it-yourself loans. When in need of a home loan, some consumers have been led to believe (by unscrupulous ads and other gimmicks), that the best way to go about choosing a lender is to shop the one with the lowest rates or the one who throws in the most freebies. But there's a little secret I've learned from years of working with all kinds of lenders: A good lender's value is *not* in their rate claims (which change daily) or program claims (which can change almost as often). Rather, a lender's *true* value is in the *level of service he provides.*

It's his reputation for follow through when your financial commitment is due and your deposit is at stake. It's someone who *says what he'll do* and then *does what he says*. The mortgage field is very competitive and many unscrupulous operators offer "pie-in-the-sky" deals to get you hooked, without the accountability to stand behind it. This is why I always counsel my clients to use a local lender who's been personally referred by someone they trust, or someone that I've worked with and wholeheartedly recommend.

When I hear a mortgage company spending big bucks running ads on the radio or in the newspaper week after week, it's a definite red flag. I'd be suspicious of any lender whose business is driven by advertising and not referrals.

There are plenty of good do-it-yourself projects, like planting a home garden or hanging curtains—but choosing a loan program is not one of them. The number of mortgage programs and plans skyrocketed over the last few years, due to the Internet. Some are fabulous for people with a certain profile but can be financially devastating for others. Frankly, it's hard even for me to keep them all straight, and I work in a "sister" business! I would never try to figure out the best mortgage program for my own personal needs. Mortgages are simply too complicated unless you do it for a living.

As with Realtors®, consumers are well-advised to find a good lender and stick with him; loyalty goes a long way. If a consumer makes a commitment to get her loan from a quality lender, that lender will shop for the best loan programs among the investors he works with, and those programs will be far better than what you can get from the outside.

Are lenders commodities? I don't think so, and neither should you!

Now, let's take a look at Realtors®. Any agent can put a sign in your yard or type your listing into the MLS—but, once again, that's not where the true value lies. The value of an experienced, savvy agent is in her knowledge, judgment, negotiating skills, and ability to manage and troubleshoot a transaction to a successful close.

In real estate, what an agent doesn't know can really hurt the consumer. Let me count the ways: I'm not a lender, but I must have a good understanding of basic mortgage principles. I'm not a real estate attorney, but because I deal with contracts all day, I must have a basic knowledge of real estate law. And I'm certainly not a home inspector, but after attending *hundreds* of home inspections over the years, I can often save my clients a lot of time by recognizing red flags in a house.

In addition, the environmental issues and regulations that I must know to advise my clients properly are staggering: lead paint, radon, mold, carbon monoxide—you name it! And today, everything must be disclosed *(something you need to keep in mind if you're trying to sell your home on your own, because in most states, disclosure requirements apply to homeowners as well as agents).*

I take my duties as a fiduciary agent very seriously because ignorance of any of these issues could greatly harm my clients. My buyer and seller clients have a substantial sum of money at stake, and if my seller-clients didn't disclose something that they should, they (and I) could get sued.

It's hard even for full-time professionals to keep up with what we must know in my industry. I do it because it's what I demand of myself as a real estate professional who takes my clients' needs seriously. Like mortgage lending, real estate is not a good-do-it-yourself project. An experienced Realtor® who can guide you through the process of buying or selling a home is no commodity. A knowledgeable, skilled agent will not only provide peace of mind, but will maximize your profits on your largest financial investment, after you pay his commission or fee. An incompetent agent is a waste of your money, no matter how cheap he is.

This is why a discount agent is no bargain. Remember, when an agent or brokerage agrees to a discount commission, he still takes all the risks inherent in being paid on contingency, but now, he gets less reward. The only way he can make this debilitating equation work is to make it up in volume. In other words, he will reduce the number and quality of his services they offer in exchange for a discounted commission. Unfortunately, what usually gets trimmed is not the fluff, but the fiduciary counsel and the personalized, hands-on attention. Instead of being there to guide you, the discount agent is usually running around prospecting for other discount listings.

Real World Example

Stan (not his real name but a real agent in my local market) is a local agent known for his discounting. He routinely cuts his commission by 1.5 to 2 percent off the going rate. It *has* worked for him in the short run—he has picked up a lot of listings, particularly from For-Sale-By-Owners because he offers such a great "deal." Because his margins are so slim, he has to make it up in volume. He is forced to provide the most limited and functionary of listing services: typing the listing into the MLS and putting a sign in the yard.

But does he advise the sellers on necessary fix-ups and how to stage their property for a quick and profitable sale? No! Does he communicate with his sellers and provide pricing counsel as the market shifts? Forget about it! Does he return calls from other agents who have questions about the home in a timely manner? Not often! Stan has good intentions, but with the deep discounts he offers that are still contingent on the sale, he just can't take the time.

Of course, we local agents know Stan's listings all too well—they're usually overpriced, and rarely in showing condition because Stan is going for volume and can't take the time to advise his so-called clients. When Stan takes a reduced commission, he's not the only one who is being discounted. The compensation offered to showing agents has also been reduced, which puts his listings at a competitive disadvantage. In truth, his listings are the last ones that we agents want to show.

Sadly, Stan's discounting won't work in the long run because his sellers receive little counsel and, therefore, his properties sit on the market and end up getting far less than they should have. Many times, Stan doesn't make a dime because his listings don't sell and the sellers end up re-listing with a quality agent. Stan is earning a "stay-away" reputation that will not only drum him out of the business but, unfortunately, will smear the image of all agents long after he's made a few bucks and gotten out of real estate.

Limited Service

No chapter on discounting would be complete without a discussion of a practice that has gained a lot of press over the last few years. MLS Entry Only has the consumer pay a licensee (it's rather silly to call this person an agent since she doesn't represent anyone) a non-refundable, flat fee to type their house information into the Multiple Listing Service. This practice has been hyped up in ads and in real estate articles as a great way for the consumer to get exposure on the MLS at a discount.

The Multiple Listing Service (MLS) has existed in one form or another since the 1920s and was designed as a co-operative among licensed agents. Prior to the MLS, agents could only show their own office's listings, so buyers were forced to go from office to office looking for the right house. There was no buyer representation, so buyers could only hope that an agent would call them if a listing came on that matched their needs. Sellers were at a tremendous disadvantage when their home only received exposure in the office where it was listed.

In today's Internet-empowered world where data is freely shared, the MLS is still a uniquely powerful marketing tool. When used by agents, the MLS brings buyers and sellers together. When each side has representation, both buyers and sellers receive the guidance and the advocacy that allow them to get the best value when they buy or sell.

Here's the rub: the MLS was designed as a professional tool between licensed agents, not as an advertising medium for the unrepresented seller. When the MLS is used as intended, agents know that they will have a licensed "partner" on the other side that will not only provide the guidance and fiduciary counsel to her own client, but also complete the many tasks that are required on both the listing and the buyer sides.

Does MLS Entry Only actually save the consumer any money? MLS Entry Only listings notoriously get fewer showings because buyer agents know they will have to deal directly with the seller and often have to do the work on both sides because there is no listing agent. Because of fewer showings, many "Entry Only" listings do not sell, forcing the seller to then hire a full-service agent and forfeit their "Entry Only" fee. Sadly, even if their home does sell, it usually does so for thousands less than it should have. The seller saved a commission, but lost far more.

Another problem with Entry Only listings is that many agents and their brokerages, understandably, do not want to take on the added liability of working with an unrepresented seller. For instance, my home state of Massachusetts is overwhelmingly an "agency" state, which means the agent is assumed to have expertise and is responsible for using that expertise to benefit the client. While the state has just added facilitator to the list of real estate relationships, this status has not yet been tested in court. Until it is, a brokerage runs a risk when it places the seller's listing in the MLS: the seller may assume that the agent is "representing" them, even if they've signed a disclosure to the contrary. Frankly, I would never want my name on a listing if I wasn't involved in negotiating and troubleshooting the transaction.

ACRE® Coach Merv Forney worked in real estate for years with his wife, Pam. They represented one of the most experienced, innovative, and professional real estate teams in Northern Virginia. Merv minces no words when it comes to limited service:

> *"I was never a Limited Service agent; I would never give up the contract-to-close responsibilities because this is where the rubber met the road, and where I could be most successful in aiding a client to close. This is the area where most transactions go wrong."*

Earlier, I talked about the types of tasks that, while important, do not necessarily need to be done by a licensed agent. If a seller wants to do some things himself to try to save money, functionary tasks are the way to go. For instance, if a seller has the time and desktop publishing software, he can certainly create his own feature sheets. If he has a digital camera, he can take his own photos and post them to a For-Sale-By-Owner website. The work may not be quite as good as an agent's (because we do it all the time and know how to showcase a property's best features), but a seller doesn't risk losing big bucks.

However, when consumers try to play Realtor® in areas such as pricing, evaluating the market, negotiating, and most importantly, troubleshooting the transaction to close, they lose. These fiduciary areas are the ones for which you want to hire a professional—because they are the ones that will make all the difference in the bottom line.

This is why MLS Entry Only is so often a rip-off. It fails precisely because it gets the process backwards. Instead of hiring a real estate professional for the vital things, like negotiating and troubleshooting the transaction, the seller pays for twenty minutes of typing. The seller is then on his own, negotiating for himself, addressing all the tasks that need to be completed for a successful close, and anticipating any potholes along the way.

In conversation with other agents, my friend and colleague, ACRE® Paula Bean, who is a 30-year real estate veteran and top producing agent in central Florida, asserts that,

> *"The biggest problem that unrepresented sellers have is with the necessary paperwork and disclosures, negotiation, and representation. So what good does it do to put a seller in the MLS, when they are then left to negotiate by themselves against a professional who does it for a living?"*

In her own unique (and humorous) way, she states further, "If that seller is going against me, they will lose any money they ever hoped to save. I will eat their lunch and have leftovers to take home to my dog."

As a child, do you remember reading the story of the *Goose Who Laid the Golden Egg* by Richard Cummings? The goose in this story would lay a golden egg each day and the farmer was getting rich. But the farmer got greedy and one day, cut open the goose in order to get to all the eggs at once. Unfortunately, his only success was in killing the goose.

The MLS (the goose) was designed as a cooperative between licensed agents who could share information for the benefit of their clients. When used as designed, the MLS has historically been the producer of lots of golden eggs—enabling sellers and buyers both to come together in a cohesive environment through their licensed representatives. But when you try to bypass the "cooperative," there are no more golden eggs.

There are reasons that states such as Texas and Illinois have established minimum service standards in real estate. This is not "restraint of trade" as some press reports would have you believe. On the contrary, this is consumer protection. As Blanche Evans of Realty Times said in her article "Are Minimum Service Rules a Disservice to Consumers?"

It's the nature of consumers to try to "beat the system" until costs have dropped to the point where the consumer is endangered. But it's not the nature of consumerism to look down the road and envision the end result of their downward pressure on fees. For instance, they don't see the day when air travel becomes unsafe because ticket prices have dropped so low that maintenance is cut or deferred.

Is Getting a Discount Really a Deal?

Have you ever bought day-old bread on the markdown table? The loaves look just like the fresh ones and you get a great price, but the minute you take a bite, you know exactly why it's discounted.

In real estate, it is much trickier to recognize that you're being discounted where it hurts because the shortfalls of using a discounter are usually not apparent until you're knee-deep in the transaction. By then, you often have to start all over again, not only losing the opportunity to make top dollar but also something that you can never get back: precious market time.

I have to quote my friend Paula Bean again, because I love how she puts things, especially in her sweet southern accent. She tells me that when a seller elects to pay by commission but wants her to cut it down, she asks him what he does for a living.

As many people are paid by salary, Paula then asks, "Let's say your boss asks that you work on Saturdays for the next month. He isn't going to pay you any more for working an extra day, and on top of that, he says he will fire you if you are unwilling to work for free for the next four Saturdays. What would you say to that?"

Most sellers respond with, "Well, I guess I would have no choice, but to do it." To which Paula replies, "Now, let me ask you this. On those Saturdays, while you're working without pay when you should be spending time with your family and friends, you may be there physically, but are you going to give your boss 100 percent effort? Would you give him 50 percent?"

I very much appreciate the consumer's concern about how costly it is to get professional real estate assistance. I make no bones about it; commissions are a very expensive way to pay for real estate assistance. If you're willing to think outside of the box, there are other options to get quality real estate guidance that will give you real value for your money. But not by asking an agent to discount her commission.

Some brokers worry that if they move to a consulting model, clients will accuse them of providing "limited service"—something that has a bad name in real estate because of the MLS Entry Only firms that provide typing and call it real estate. The problem is, these firms limit their offerings to the services you could handle yourself. The consulting model, however, limits the agent's services to the pieces that draw on her real expertise—the ones that would be hard for a non-professional to do on your own.

Limited service, in and of itself, is not a bad thing; sometimes, it's what the consumer needs. I call it CHOICE. Sometimes a seller finds his own buyer—and I think that as matchmaking services on sites such as Craig's List continue to proliferate—that this will happen more and more. The seller doesn't NEED a full service package—he NEEDS help in negotiating and troubleshooting, and getting the sale to close with an expert's counsel and care.

Our industry's refusal to provide this "limited service" doesn't eliminate this need. It simply throws these sellers into the arms of attorneys (who can't do this as well as we can and often charge twice as much) or leaves them without any help (which causes them to lose a lot of money). Just because a seller wants to do her own feature sheets or digital photography—shouldn't mean that she has to do without an agent's negotiating and troubleshooting skills!

Homeowners who have to make remodeling decisions may be desperate for the knowledge that a real estate pro can offer. A few hundred dollars spent for a couple of hours of consulting would be money well spent to ensure they were making the right decisions. Does the industry's refusal to provide this "limited service" take away this need? No, but the consumer loses because he often puts his money in the wrong places and it shows up a few years later when he goes to sell.

Unassisted buyers often fall in love with a FSBO (For-Sale-By-Owner) and would be glad to pay a professional for a few hours of help in negotiating an offer and making sure everything is in place so they don't lose their deposit or the house. And wouldn't the FSBO be happy to have that fee included in the transaction, especially since it would be a much more reasonable cost than the standard co-brokerage? Who loses when we don't offer this "limited service?" The buyer does, the FSBO often does, and the real estate industry certainly does; we've lost untold amounts of money over the years because we don't offer choices.

The real estate industry by and large thinks that if we "don't give in", that people will be forced into a full package, paid by commission. I'm sorry—those days are over!. In the Internet world, there are a growing number of alternatives. While the alternatives may not be nearly as good as using a real estate professional, our refusal to address these needs only sends the public elsewhere.

No matter what you choose, you as a buyer or seller should have the right to make informed choices. The heart of consulting is listening to the consumer's needs and then presenting alternatives. Our job, as professionals, should be to help you sort out the plusses and minuses of each alternative.

Real Estate and the Internet

I ORIGINALLY WROTE PARTS OF THIS CHAPTER FOR A BOOK I coauthored with my wonderful colleague, Ken Deshaies, a few years back titled *How To Make Your Realtor® Get You the Best Deal: Massachusetts Edition*. I've added some material to it here, but the message has only grown in importance and is worth repeating now more than ever.

> *Despite advertising claims to the contrary, the Internet is not an experienced real estate professional. It cannot consult, counsel, advise, apply knowledge of local real estate laws and market conditions, make judgments, own the result, or most importantly, understand your individual goals and needs and care about you as a client. Furthermore, while the Internet can provide information, it cannot interpret it.*

As the Internet continues to grow from an information resource to an expedient platform for all types of commerce, it is vital to look at what technology can and cannot do. This differentiation is especially crucial when dealing with real estate, an environment where online companies increasingly clutter your inbox with ads and schemes that claim to save you incredible amounts of money and time. Sift through this morass of information, deals, and promises with a careful eye!

I want to be very clear that technology—and specifically the Internet—is a wonderful thing! Technology is a fabulous way to gather data and can do certain functionary tasks better, faster, and cheaper than any human being ever could. But the danger is that by itself, the Internet can never provide the fiduciary counsel required in services such as mortgage lending, law, and real estate.

Functionary/fiduciary—why do I keep using these "f" words? If you're to get the best value in real estate, it's crucial to understand the difference between the real estate data you find online and the advice, counsel, and interpretation of that data that only a Realtor® can provide.

Information Versus Knowledge

I consider myself an Internet savvy Realtor®. In 1995, I was one of the first agents in the nation to develop a real estate website and have never looked back. I built my business online and continue to stay on the forefront of cutting-edge technology. I am proud to be one of only 200 Cyberstars®, an elite group of Realtors® who generate a significant portion of their business through the use of current technology.

Over the years, my real estate team has generated a significant portion of our new business online. I'm a believer in the use of Internet technology to encourage a free flow of information from us to the consumer. And I'm not alone. You will find that a growing breed of Internet-savvy Realtors® are now offering technology and tools that provide the most complete sources of real estate information anywhere.

I'm proud that my own team's real estate site (www.TheHome-Consultants.com) has been nationally recognized over the years for the depth of its content, and yet I've had many of my "old school" colleagues over the years question why we freely give out so much information. They have often said, "If you give out too much information, buyers and sellers will have no reason to call you."

I flatly disagree. Although my team provides an abundance of information, we have never had a shortage of requests to retain our services. This experience is replicated nationally. *The 2007 NAR Profile of Home Buyers and Sellers* found that while 79 percent of buyers used the Internet to search for homes, 4 out of 5 of those buyers turned to a Realtor® when it was time to actually purchase a home. That's because there's a big difference between information and knowledge.

John Tuccillo writes in *The Eight New Rules of Real Estate*, "Information is a collection of facts or observations about reality. Knowledge is actionable." In today's information age, consumers can increasingly get all the information they want or need, but that data can be financially or personally misleading—unless someone with expertise can interpret that knowledge so you can act on it correctly.

Information, without the context of a professional who can share the day-to-day knowledge of the industry, is just data. If a consumer were to act on it without context, you could reach incorrect conclusions and achieve undesirable results.

Information is like sand on a beach—it's plentiful and anyone can find it. But if you want to build a sand castle, you may want to consult the Sandmaster who lives on the beach. She can tell you how much water to use, what weather conditions are best for building, and most importantly, when the tide comes in. Without this knowledge, you could spend an entire afternoon building a great sand castle, only to have it washed away too soon.

Myths Involving Real Estate and the Internet

As noted above, people love to surf the Internet for real estate. However, there are myths about what the Internet can and cannot do. You may have heard people say,

"The Internet is great! I can . . .

1. Buy a book
2. Buy an airline ticket
3. Buy or sell a house
4. Get legal advice
5. Receive a medical opinion

. . . all online!"

When did that list cross from fact to myth? If you said after number two, the airline ticket, give yourself a gold star!

Books and plane tickets are commodities bought mostly by price. But the last three are services that require counsel, advice, knowledge, and an understanding of your individual needs. The first two are functionary products, te last three are fiduciary services.

You can purchase the first two products entirely online and probably save money in the process. For the last three services, the Internet is a great place to become educated and start your search for service providers. But if you try to "go it alone" with just the data you find online, you will very likely risk losing your shirt (or your health)—unless you consult a local provider who understands your individual needs and is accountable for his services.

Let's look at a couple of obvious examples before turning to real estate. Let's say there's an online site called "WeKnowLaws.com". For $39.95, payable in advance by credit card, you can receive a "legal opinion." Does this opinion come from an attorney, a paralegal, or a truck driver? The site says it's from an attorney, but how do we know for sure? And what if you take this legal advice and your case turns out poorly? How do you get out of the deeper legal dilemma in which you now find yourself?

Local attorneys who are dependent on referrals for future business have a great incentive to stand behind their advice and counsel. Does anyone at "WeKnowLaws.com" care if you're unhappy with her opinion? In other words, what happens if something goes wrong?

Another example are the online mortgage companies that advertise everywhere. If you've read the business section of the paper, you know that many of these companies are struggling. Why?

First, with differing state laws and local procedures, much of the mortgage process must still be done locally—so there's little economy to doing the process online. More importantly, many consumers are finally catching on that those interest rates and financing programs are often connected to scams.

Do you really think for a moment that an online mortgage company in Dot-Com-Land is particularly concerned if you're unhappy with their services? A good mortgage lender derives much of his business from local Realtors® and the community. He has to make the situation right for his clients if he wants repeat business. In other words, he must be *accountable*! But the national dot-com mortgage companies do not.

> On a local level, you'll find that the best service providers, whether they are lenders, attorneys, or real estate agents, get the bulk of their business from referrals. You'll know who they are because they don't advertise very much. They don't have to! Conversely, be wary of service providers who spend big bucks advertising; you want someone whose primary source of business is referrals from happy clients, not advertising.

Use the Internet to educate yourself on the mortgage process and compare different rates and programs. Then take that information and the best lending packages you can find to a local, recommended lender. Ask if she can match it. If the offer is legitimate, either she will match it, or tell you why she can't.

Have you ever been to a medical website? There are many wonderful sites out there for the medical consumer, such as the objective-information sites WebMD.com and MDChoice.com. If you were to visit one of these sites to become a more educated patient, and then take your questions and concerns to your doctor, that would be a smart use of the Internet. If, however, you were to visit a site and attempt to diagnose yourself, the results could be disastrous.

A Closer Look at the Internet and Real Estate

As I've pointed out, real estate combines functionary tasks with fiduciary counsel. Functionary tasks, such as property searches or accessing home sales data, can be done cheaper, faster, and better online. If that were the whole of real estate, I would be the first to applaud the ever-growing number of national dot-coms promising to provide you these services right from your own computer. But unfortunately, many of these online services want you to believe that what you would get emailed is the same thing with the same value as what you get from a local real estate professional—and that's simply not true.

To illustrate, let's take a detailed look at home valuation companies. These websites heavily advertise that they will send you a free online home valuation. All you have to do is give them a street address and the free valuation is yours. So what do you get? (Drum roll, please.) A list of homes sold within a one-mile radius of that address. That's it.

Does this "home valuation," coming from a national site, take into account the power plant going in two blocks away from this home that will ultimately affect its value? Has it seen the home's interior to find out how it compares with others? Does it take into account the railroad tracks on the next street?

What about the local economy and the fact that young professionals are starting to move into the area, accelerating a probable increase in prices? What about sewer abatements or the newest regulations? How about the cities and towns that are developing "over-55" communities and are increasingly earmarking the town's tax money there rather than in the schools? A national dot-com that is emailing some sales data to a seller can't advise them of the things that could greatly affect the value of their property! So who can? A local Realtor® who knows the local market.

In the last few years, online sites such as Zillow.com claim to let you see what an agent sees. Zillow was launched a few years back to great fanfare. CNN Money even said it was time to "Say good-bye to appraisers and possibly real estate agents."

As it turns out, this service isn't new, but simply a twist on the same old online home valuations. Meaning: plug in a property address, it will spit out your home's "market value." These websites come with a lot of bells and whistles, such as impressive rooftop satellite photos and assigning a "value" to all the homes, whether or not they're for sale.

But are these "values" accurate? Well, sometimes, you luck out and they are amazingly close and sometimes they are so far off, it's laughable. Why is that? The site uses public data from the property's city or town, and that is the problem. Some cities and towns do regular appraisals and are fairly up-to-date, while others are way behind. The accuracy of this data is further compromised because many homeowners will put additions on their home or do major upgrades without telling their municipality, in order to avoid higher taxes.

Often, tax records on recently sold properties will not reflect their true sales price. That is because the "considerations" in the sale are not always taken into consideration. For example, some sales include personal items that will inflate the sales price, such as large appliances or expensive window treatments. Sometimes the sales price is artificially high because the buyer is getting money back for closing costs. For all these reasons, we agents know that public records are only a starting point.

The service, however, does give the consumer an opportunity to add information that may not be reflected in the tax data. That's helpful if the homeowner is truthful, objective, and has the knowledge to assign the proper values. But this can be very difficult for the average consumer. I have seen homeowners refer to an unfinished room in the basement, without a closet or windows, as a "bedroom." Now the owners might claim to have a four-bedroom home rather than a three-bedroom. A national online service would value this home and a true four-bedroom as equals, when they are clearly not.

I've seen owners put tens of thousands of dollars into adding beautiful in-ground pools with cabanas in their backyards. If you plug that pool as an upgrade into a national site, it will add a lot of "value"—because in some parts of the country, like Florida, a pool actually adds value. But in the Northeast, where I live, because of the shorter summer season, a pool is a liability to at least 50 percent of buyers.

The value of an upgrade has a lot to do with the neighborhood where it's located (more on this later). An expensive kitchen upgrade with high-end cabinetry and granite counters may be a wonderful update for a home in an upscale neighborhood, but the "value" of that remodel would be considerably less in a working-class area. If a consumer does not have a background in real estate, how would he know how to value his upgraded kitchen?

Zillow refers to its website as a "Kelley Blue Book for homes." But homes are not automobiles. When new models are introduced into the market, they have an objective value with a calculated depreciation.

Homes, on the other hand, are unique. Where is the property situated? Is it close to the street or on a corner lot with lots of traffic? Are the expensive moldings and faux fireplace mantle really an upgrade to the majority of buyers, or so unique to that owner's taste that it may actually hurt its market value? How does an owner, without an intimate knowledge of the market, put a price on aesthetics? On a national valuation site, an ugly home with little landscaping and no curb appeal will be priced the same as one that draws buyers like bees to honey.

Valuing homes accurately for their local market is what experienced Realtors® do every day. With knowledge of the local market and familiarity with what does and does not add value, we can objectively look at real estate property and factor in all the "intangibles" that a national online service can't possibly get right.

The Internet Is Evolution, Not Revolution, for Realtors® Services

Over the last fifteen years as the Internet gained steam, prognosticators predicted it would eliminate the need for Realtors® in the transaction. However, a research survey conducted by the Journal of Information Technology* stated:

Computers and the Internet have been billed as enabling new ways of doing business. The expectation was that real estate agents would go away once consumers could see all the home listing information, but that has not happened. Instead, as the amount of real estate information has exploded, it has required more professionals to be involved in supporting, understanding, and processing that information.

The adoption of technology clearly has provided access to information such as listings, mortgage rates, and neighborhood demographics, previously unavailable to consumers. That increase in the quantity of available information has led to better quality information which, in turn, has led to better informed consumers. Armed with more information, consumers have demanded more specialized services as well as better service from real estate agents.

*Redefining Access: Uses and Roles of Information and Communication Technologies in the U.S. Residential Real Estate Industry from 1995 to 2005.

Peter G. Miller is also known as OurBroker®, and is the author of six real estate books—including *The Common-Sense Mortgage*—and the original creator and host of America Online's Real Estate Center. He once wrote in Realty Times about why the Internet has not replaced Realtors® after all:

> *According to the National Association of Realtors ®, 85 percent of all homes were sold through the brokerage system in 2005. Of the rest, 11 percent were For-Sale-By-Owner (FSBO) sales; 1 percent first listed with a broker and then sold by themselves; 1 percent sold to a home-buying company and 2 percent sold in "other" ways.*

> *Ten years earlier—before the emergence of the Internet—the percentage of successful FSBOs was actually larger. NAR figures show that 81 percent of all homes were sold by brokers in 1995. That same*

year 15 percent were FSBO sales, 2 percent involved home-buying companies and 2 percent were "other."

These results are notable because the Internet was supposed to do away with the need for brokers, or to at least reduce their role to a sort of clerical activity worth at most a few hundred dollars per transaction.

The problem with such predictions, and the reason for their failure, is that homes are not stocks, bonds, or airline tickets. A hundred shares of IBM are exactly the same as any other hundred shares — it makes no difference which hundred shares you own. Houses are all different. Every property has an inherent physical nature and few buyers are willing to miss an in-person, tactile examination of a property before making the massive financial and psychological commitment real estate transactions require.

Yet companies, both online and off, continue to mislead the public about what the Internet can do and where an agent's value lies. This is bad enough when it's a third-party company trying to "cash in" by tapping into the public's "do-it-yourself" mentality, but it is particularly dangerous when it comes from a real estate brokerage that ought to know better. Here's an advertisement that has run for years on the radio in my local market in Boston:

The Internet has certainly changed real estate. With access to listings, buyers can do a lot of an agent's work for them. So if buyers are doing most of the work, why haven't real estate commissions come down? At "Home Discount Realty," we think that if you're doing the work, you should be rewarded! In fact, if you buy a home with us, our agents will rebate to you 25 percent of their commission when you close.

To suggest that because buyers are able to educate themselves on the current housing inventory, the agent is doing less and should be compensated less, is ludicrous. While it is absolutely true that technology allows buyers to do their own narrowing down of properties, this is not where the value of an experienced agent lies. As I pointed out earlier, a buyer agent's value is not in finding the home, but in getting the best deal for their buyer-clients once it is found.

Clearly, technology has saved agents from doing manual home searches and being the "gatekeeper" of information. Instead, the average agent today is spending more time than ever servicing her clients. Rather than doing manual searches and drive-bys of properties, today's buyer agent is checking out tax records and digging into the history of homes that are of interest to the buyer. Thirty years ago, it was "buyer beware," but today it is "buyer be represented." And the onus is on the agent to make sure there are no "surprises."

Think about the following scenario:

A friend of yours isn't feeling well so she makes an appointment with her doctor. Before the appointment, she goes online and researches all the diseases or maladies that possibly match her symptoms. Imagine her walking into the doctor's office and announcing to her doctor that since she's done so much of the "legwork" of gathering information, the doctor's job is reduced, and therefore, the doctor should be paid less.

Your friend has honored herself by becoming a more educated patient. And the treatment the doctor prescribes may be easier for her because she may know what to expect. Yet she hasn't even begun to done her doctor's job. That's because a good physician's value is *not in gathering medical information, but in interpreting it and applying it to thr individual patient's case.*

In real estate, when a home buyer becomes educated about the real estate process and the types of homes that might fit his needs, he helps his agent to help him—but he isn't doing the agent's job, no mater what the ads say. Realtors® put in as many, if not more, hours into each transaction as they did fifteen years ago. Our time now is just spent differently.

I should point out that all the great technology not only fails to save a good agent any net time on a transaction, but it has greatly driven up the average agent's expenses. I am particularly frustrated with discount realty firms that undermine their own industry's worth in ads like these, to try to gain a competitive edge.

One more word to the wise on these ads: I can guarantee you that agents willing to hand back 25 percent of their compensation on transaction that are still contingent on the sale will not be the seasoned pros who will hammer out the best deal for buyers. A quality agent knows that she's giving the consumer good value for his money. The quality of negotiation and troubleshooting of the transaction makes that abundantly clear. An agent willing to hand back a quarter of her income is essentially saying, 'My services are overpriced for what I will give you so I will give you a rebate.'

I wrote this chapter to help the real estate consumer use the Internet effectively for what it does best—gather information and become a more educated consumer. Again I'll say it: the Internet cannot replace an experienced Realtor®. There is lot more to successfully buying and selling a home than just viewing property listings and pursuing current sales data. Simply accessing housing inventory without interpreting it based on a buyer's needs, goals, and timetable is not going to get the client his best value any more than an online market analysis emailed to a seller is going to get him the best value when he sells.

WHY CAN'T THE CONSUMER HAVE BOTH?

IN A RECENT ARTICLE in RIS Magazine, Brian Buffini, founder and chairman of Buffini & Company, made a very interesting observation: although 80-90% of real estate buyers start their home search online, almost none would actually go to the next step and click "Add to Shopping Cart."

Online technology gives you a running start. But to cross the finish line, you need a flesh-and-blood Realtor® who knows the local market.

The problem is that traditional real estate companies and associations are still telling the public that if they want the hands-on personal care that Buffini advocates, the full-service commission-only model is the only option. Those who want to take advantage of the do-it-yourself opportunities (and cost savings) or who do want full service, but just don't like paying by commission—are turned away.

On the other hand, third-party companies that advertise that their sites and services can replace a good real estate professional are also missing the boat; technology can provide lots of data, but without a pro to interpret what it means, you can lose thousands on your largest asset.

For instance, while Zillow clearly states that its "zestimate" is just a starting point and is not an appraisal, the message isn't always getting through—we agents are continually running into self-described "zillow-ites" who argue with our price analysis of their home, saying the "zestimate" came in much higher (and more to their liking). Lending Tree continually advertises that when "lenders compete, you win" encouraging the mindset that lenders are commodities to be shopped by price and clearly sending the message that cheaper is better. Discount real estate firms, promising a big rebate if you use one of "their" agents, are sending the same message about real estate agents.

These messages are creating "falsely empowered consumers": people who think they know a lot more than they do, and who are at risk of losing thousands of dollars and hundreds of hours.

Lenders and agents, like other fiduciaries such as CPAs, financial planners, or attorneys are not commodities. The quality of their service, level of expertise, talent and experience can make a huge difference in whether you get good value and peace of mind with your loan, purchase, or sale—or get financially hung out to dry.

A real estate consultant can provide that crucial middle ground: harnessing the incredible power of the Internet to allow those consumers that have the time and desire to market or find their own homes to do so, while offering the vital fiduciary contract-to-close duties. The consultant can also provide choices in how clients pay her.

The statistics are clear: agent-assisted properties net far more than those that are sold entirely by owner, even after paying the agent's commission or fee. USA Today's 2003 study found agent-assisted properties netted 21% more; the National Association of Realtors® 2006 Home Buyer and Seller Survey found that agent-assisted properties netted 23% more. The bottom line is that having a real estate professional on your side will save you far more than it costs.

The trick is using the technology of the Internet to provide access and compile data, while bringing in a real estate professional to interpret all that data and handle the contract-to-close responsibilities that are so vital if you're to get the best deal when you buy or sell a home, or make other real estate decisions.

Misleading Advertising

Cutting Through the Hype

SINCE THE BEGINNING OF TIME, advertising has been used to sell products and services. While few advertisers outright lie, many often mislead because they don't tell the whole story. Real estate consumers today are particularly vulnerable to half-truths because they're increasingly frustrated with the lack of flexibility: only one service package, and only one way to pay for it. Real estate looks deceptively simple—until you're knee-deep into your transaction.

These four ads, while fictional, are based on real ones in print, radio, and television. By now, these might elicit a chuckle or two, as well as alert your "consumer rip-off radar" to the danger of losing time and money.

Some Ads

AD #1 in the Newspaper
We'll sell your home for only $2995! We advertise your home.
We show your home to buyers. We do everything!
And of course, we only get paid for results.
Full Service
While Saving Money!
Contact We-Promise-You-The-World Realty
555-555-5555.

THE TRUTH: That $2995 fee does not include the Multiple Listing Service (MLS)—or compensation to the buyer's agent . Of course, they'll tell you that's because they're marketing directly to the buyer, not to the agents.

This ad looks deceptively like straight fee-for-service except for one little detail: they only get paid for results. Sounds great, but what does it really mean to you, the consumer? You'll certainly get a sign in your front yard, but how much will they proactively advertise and promote your home when they're not even assured of getting a fee? What quality of agents work for fees that are still contingent on the sale?

Unless it's a torrid seller's market with a tremendous shortage of inventory, your home needs to be listed on the MLS if you want to sell for top dollar. Serious, qualified buyers overwhelmingly work with an agent. And those agents will avoid bringing your home to the attention of those buyers.

This advertisement is also a classic bait-and-switch. After you've had your home on the market for a month or so without MLS exposure, you're probably going to inquire if they provide MLS "at a discount." Of course they do! They will then offer you a discount commission (so much for the fee concept), but they don't take the whole hit themselves, they also discount the compensation offered to the agent bringing the buyer (again, reducing the likelihood of that agent showing your home).

It would be great if all agents were selfless souls who never looked at their compensation when showing homes, but this is one of the conundrums that today's agent faces. Few buyers have the cash available to pay their agent themselves, so agents working with buyers have to depend on compensation from the listing agent (called a "co-broke," in real estate lingo). Yes, most agents put their buyer's interest first, but if they have a choice between earning the going compensation and the discounted compensation, which home are they going to show? Surely not the discounted home.

AD #2 on the Radio

Jake:	Hey, Jane, did you hear about that cool website, I-Did-Myself-In.com sponsored by We-Get-All-Our-Business-From-Ads Mortgage? Sellers can put their home on this super duper website and pay no real estate commission!
Jane:	I sure did, Jake! My friend Susie told me that she had her home listed with an agent for six months with no

| | showings, but once she listed her home on I-Did-Myself-In.com she had an offer in one day! She saved $12,000! |
| **Jake:** | Of course, if you're looking to buy or refinance, make sure you call We-Get-All-Our-Business-From-Ads Mortgage. Rates have never been lower and we're open on weekends! |

THE TRUTH: We-Get-All-Our-Business-From-Ads Mortgage doesn't care if these homes sell or not. Their primary interest is in selling mortgages to buyers calling about the listings. Their secondary interest is in selling extras to these sellers such as yard signs, "enhanced" exposure on their website, and ads in their print magazines, because the seller doesn't have a listing agent.

This ad would lead you to believe that all you have to do is list your home on their site and your house sells! If Jane's friend really had her home listed on the MLS and didn't get a showing, I can guarantee you that her home was significantly overpriced (probably because she used a discount broker), and she re-priced it to market before listing it on I-Did-Myself-In.com.

Real sellers who have used similar super-duper, go-it-alone websites will tell you a very different story. We know because not only has our team shown many of these "By Owner" homes, but we have also assisted our buyer-clients in purchasing homes from these sellers. Overwhelmingly, the website doesn't sell these homes, we agents do. That's because, far from saving a full commission, the sellers were only too happy to pay our fee for bringing them a qualified buyer who's been educated about the market, especially after having to play real estate agent for a few weeks (or months).

If this isn't bad enough, this particular company does a little bait-and-switch routine as well, raising deceit to a whole new level. First, they ensnare the do-it-yourself seller with ads describing how easy it is to sell a house, and how with their super-duper website, they can sell directly to buyers and save the whole commission. Then, after the seller has dropped a bunch of money buying add-ons, as well as ads in the paper, with no bites, they then actually instruct these sellers to mass e-mail real estate agents, inviting them to bring their buyers.

Of course, after first having their profession belittled by these ads, and then getting spammed, most agents aren't chomping at the bit to show these homes (unless it's a seller's market with a tremendous shortage of inventory).

I'll say it again: Legitimate mortgage companies with good reputations get the lion's share of their business from real estate professionals who recommend them because they offer great service and are accountable. Why do you think that We-Get-All-Our-Business-From-Ads-Mortgage would choose to spend thousands of dollars per week running ads that alienate real estate? They gave up on getting business from agents a long time ago—because their service is so terrible that no agent would recommend them.

AD #3 on the Radio

> My neighbors just sold their house. Boy, were they jealous when I told them that I just listed mine with ABC Discount Realty. ABC only charges $500 to put me in the Multiple Listing Service. Now, I have thousands of agents working for me!

THE TRUTH: This seller has no one working for her. And in all probability, she's just thrown $500 away. As was pointed out earlier, "MLS Entry Only" is a huge consumer rip-off because the MLS was not designed as an advertising medium for For-Sale-By-Owner homes.

Again, unless there is a tremendous shortage of inventory, most agents will do everything within their power to avoid showing these listings. Not only is there legal liability in dealing directly with the seller, but the agent is often roped into not only providing services to their buyers, but also doing the work of the missing listing agent. Because of the decreased exposure, even if the home sells, it will usually do so for thousands of dollars less than it should have.

AD #4 on Television

> **Voice over:** Want to find out how much your home is worth?
>
> Don't want to deal with pushy salespeople?
>
> Just go to FreeHomeValue.com and a trained professional will provide a free analysis of what your home will sell for in today's market. It's that easy!

THE TRUTH: There are two types of valuation services. Comparative Market Analyses (CMAs) done by computer, and those done by agents. As was discussed earlier, the computer generated ones are fairly useless. This ad, on the other hand, touts the benefits of a CMA researched and prepared by an agent (hoping to get your listing because they're working for *free*). What this company is implying, of course, is that by going through them, you're not getting a "pushy salesperson," but rather a "trained professional."

Here are the facts. What you're really getting by going through this online service is an agent who's willing to pay this outfit for leads (that's you, as soon as you fill out the online form). The company sets itself up as the middleman, making their money off agents, while providing zero added value to you, the consumer.

Let's think this through logically. Who's more likely to be the pushy salesperson? The agent who you contact, either because of their good reputation or because they were referred, or the agents who call you because they've paid big bucks for your lead? Who is more likely to be a quality professional? An agent who receives the majority of their business by referral? Or someone who is so desperate for business that he pays a dot-com for leads?

It should be very clear to you that I understand the consumer's desire to get honest value for their money. I know that many consumers today are looking for alternatives to a rigid commission system. But the answer does not lie in discount brokers offering reduced service, because they will cost you more in the long run. They are hucksters offering pie-in- the-sky deals and are not going to do much, other than separate you from your money.

The Unrepresented Seller
(Better Known as For-Sale-By-Owner)

Get the Facts

WHY DIDN'T I CALL THIS CHAPTER, "FOR-SALE-BY-OWNER"? Because For-Sale-By-Owner is misleading. Think about it. Anyone who owns a property and wants to sell it, is in fact, a For-Sale-By-Owner seller. The owner holds the title. It's just a matter of how much professional assistance he wants.

It's common for agents to say, "I sold this home" or to ask another agent, "How many homes did you sell last year?" But agents do not sell homes! Rather, agents manage the transaction, provide expert services, and most importantly, offer *vital counsel, representation, and advocacy*.

The term For-Sale-By-Owner, or FSBO, is a response to the real estate industry's historical all-or-nothing structure. Traditionally, if you were a homeowner wishing to sell your home, you either hired an agent for a full package of "stuff" (even if you did not need some of that "stuff" or if you just wanted the counsel and guidance) or you went it totally alone.

Over the last few years, more choices have emerged, such as discount brokers and other third party companies—both online and off—offering an array of functionary-type services at bargain basement prices, sometimes for free. But neither the traditional real estate industry, nor the discounters are telling you the whole story. The traditional broker is saying that in order to get counsel and representation, you have to buy the whole package of services and you can only pay by commission. She doesn't tell you that you may not need some of the services—or that you could pay in a different way and still get what you do need.

On the other side, the discounters and the myriad of third-party companies that have popped up to feed off the "do-it-yourselfer" aren't telling you the full story either. Simply throwing your home on the MLS without market or pricing counsel, or having your home on their super-duper website, isn't likely going to get your home sold, certainly not for the best value. They also won't tell you that although today's technology can perform functionary tasks better and cheaper than any human being, technology cannot provide the fiduciary counsel, advocacy, and day-to-day market knowledge that can make all the difference to your bottom line.

Do-It-Yourself companies will tell you that you can save thousands of dollars on commissions, but they won't tell you that you can lose thousands more. This loss is in the ultimate price you get for your home as well as all the other "nickel and dime" marketing costs that quickly add up. Nor will they tell you that you can lose something else that you can never get back—your precious market time.

If you're like most home sellers I've spoken with, you want straight answers, plain and simple. In other words, you want honest value for your dollar. Paying only for tasks and services you require, and receiving the counsel that you need, makes a lot more sense than paying a convoluted percentage of your home's sale price.

If you're currently trying, or planning, to sell your home without representation, this chapter is for you. And though my background is as an agent and broker, I want to be very clear: my goal is not to talk you out of selling your own home. Rather, it is to make sure that you are informed about the whole process and the other options you may have, before plunking down thousands of dollars on useless services, as well as wasting hours of your time on unproductive work.

If after looking over the information in this chapter, you believe that you are OK without professional real estate assistance—more power to you. But if you want vital fiduciary counsel, and you are flexible with how to pay for quality services, you may want to look at working with a trained and certified real estate consultant.

You May Beat the Odds, but Know Them Going In

You own a home. You know the sacrifice it takes and the rewards that it brings. It was probably the largest purchase you ever made. It is now your largest asset and, if you've owned it for more than a few years, even with the ups and downs of the market, its value has probably still increased far faster than any other investment you've made.

It is understandable and very human to want to keep the profit you've earned. Every year, particularly in a seller's market, some homeowners decide to try to sell their home without assistance. Before you start spending serious money on ads and For-Sale-By-Owner websites and spending serious time holding numerous open houses to strangers, know what you're up against.

The actual success rate of unrepresented sellers in selling their own homes is difficult to measure because it seems the only organization willing to put anything in writing is the National Association of Realtors® (NAR) through their Home Buyer and Seller Survey.

One piece of data that is backed up by a survey in writing is the NAR Home Buyer and Seller Survey for 2009. This survey shows that of all sales in 2009, 85% were sold with agent assistance and 11% were sold without assistance.

These are fairly long odds. But the biggest risk you take when trying to sell on your own is not whether you can actually close a deal. As long as you don't spend a lot of non-refundable money trying, get expert help with the paperwork and other legal issues, and, most importantly, take the necessary precautions to safeguard your home and family, it doesn't hurt to try, especially if you are not in any hurry to sell.

Although the close rate for unassisted sellers is low, the risk to sellers in trying to sell without assistance is not that you will fail to sell your own home without help. **The real risk to sellers is that you may succeed but lose more than you save.**

Lew Sichelman, in his syndicated article, "FSBOs (For Sale by Owners) may be LM (Losing Millions)," printed in major papers across the country, said,

> This is the case of the missing 10%. It's a tale of lost millions, and it stars the thousands of owners who sell their own homes without professional help.
>
> It seems that in their desire to save the 5% or 6% fee that real estate brokers charge for their services, FSBOs (as in For Sale By Owners) earn 16% less than owners of comparable homes who put the transaction into the hands of an experienced agent, according to a survey conducted by none other than the National Association of Realtors®. (emphasis added)

Before we delve into what the above really means, let's first check out the source that Mr. Sichelman quotes, which I mentioned earlier. I was a member of the National Association of Realtors® for years, but at first glance even I would question its objectivity. Even though my team's experiences with hundreds of sellers very much confirms this finding, as an MBA with a business mindset, I like to check out my sources.

The NAR commissions a fairly extensive annual survey, "The Profile of Home Buyers and Sellers." In the 2009 survey, NAR sent an eight-page questionnaire to 120,038 consumers who bought or sold a home between July of 2008 and June of 2009. The survey yielded 9,138 usable responses (a very respectable, and statistically significant, 7.9 percent response rate). It is my understanding that an independent firm tallies and verifies the results.

While we would all agree that the NAR survey may not be the most objective source, given its public profile, it's extremely doubtful that the NAR would risk distributing false results. As a major trade organization, it simply wouldn't publicize the findings.

Yet there is another, more independent source. A few years back, USA Today printed the results of their study "Agents Net More." The survey results were part of an article, "For-Sale-by- Owner Can Be a Hard Sell—Agents often Worth Their Weight in Commission," written by Joyce Cohen.

Still, I would prefer to confirm these numbers with surveys commissioned by the FSBO company side. Although there are plenty of claims from For-Sale-By-Owner organizations, I could not find one that could back up their claims with any hard numbers. Most will explain that it's because they are not real estate agents and therefore are legally prohibited from taking part in the actual sales transaction of any of the properties they advertise. This makes it difficult for them to track how many of their properties sell and how quickly. Hmmm… this seems to be a rather interesting excuse for not providing statistics to back up their advertising claims. Is there a legal reason to stop them from commissioning a survey of the sellers using their services?

Instead, they try to undermine the validity of unfavorable surveys. For instance, Colby Sambrotto of ForSaleByOwner.com disputes the results of surveys showing the dollars-and-cents advantage of using a Realtor®. "It just doesn't jibe with our experience," he says. "We haven't put together a big study," he concedes. "But we ask all of our sellers if they were successful and 65% say they were. And we ask if they sold at or near their asking price, and 85% say they do."

With all the ad claims by various FSBO companies, it seems that none have put their money where their mouth is and commissioned their own survey. And why not? They certainly have the bucks and the incentive, and many of these For-Sale-By-Owner organizations are backed by financial entities that would like nothing better than to take over a major part of the real estate industry. If their claims of big savings are really true, it seems logical that if they had hard numbers they would be happy to publicize them.

Is the reason they haven't commissioned surveys because they know that the results won't back up their advertising claims?

What Does This Mean?

The USA Today survey shows agent-assisted properties selling for 21.49 percent more than For-Sale-By-Owner homes in 2003. In 2009, the Home Buyer and Seller Survey showed Realtor®-assisted properties selling for 25% percent more. As a seller, you should be aware of these numbers before you plunk down your hard-earned money. The truth is that even though commissions can be an expensive way to pay for real estate services, you could pay a 10 percent commission and still walk away with far more in your pocket than selling on your own, not to speak of all the work you would still have to do with the energy, effort, and added liability that work entails.

For example, a few years ago I received a call from a seller that I had spoken with a few years back. She triumphantly told me that she was able to sell her home on her own and, even with paying the agent that brought her a buyer, she still saved $10,000 in commissions. I asked her what price she got for her home and she told me $350,000. Here's the kicker: I know her home and her neighborhood well, and I'm fairly confident that had my team listed her house, we could have gotten her $400,000 for her home. So she saved $10,000 in commissions but lost $50,000 in the ultimate sales price. To add insult to injury, this seller ended up paying her real estate attorney double for doing the needed tasks that a listing agent would have done. That's why when talking with sellers who are considering selling on their own, I always stress: *It's not what you save, it's what you keep!*

My colleague, Paula Bean, says,

> *Home sellers do not know what they do not know. In other words, they do not know what they have lost in price. They do not know what they have lost when negotiation time comes. They do not know what is typical and normal on home inspections, so they do not know what they have lost there. They don't know which lenders are reputable and which are not. There is really no way for them to compare what some of the FSBO companies state. I usually ask a prospective client who is balking at how much they pay me, "What are you more concerned with? How much money you have in your pocket when this is all over or how much you want to pay me to make it happen?"*

There are a myriad of reasons that Realtor®-assisted properties net far more than those sold by their owner. They include the proper pricing and positioning of a home for the town and neighborhood, the extensive ability to market through a vast network of agents and their buyers, providing objective negotiating of price and terms, and most importantly, the expertise to troubleshoot the transaction so it closes.

I'm done with my warnings. My purpose is not to try to talk anyone out of selling on your own but rather to make sure that you are informed about the entire process and your odds of success before you start. In addition, as we'll see in a later chapter, you have alternative ways to get the quality services and representation that will let you keep more of your hard-earned money when the deal is done.

If you are still going to try selling on your own, make sure you read about The Four Financial Potholes later in this book:

1. Pricing
2. Contracts, Disclosures, and Paperwork
3. Negotiations
4. Troubleshooting the Transaction

This is where sellers lose money when going it alone. Knowledge is power, and if you are going to sell your home on your own, pay special attention to the places where you could lose serious cash. Later, I'll also cover how you can avoid these problem areas for very little money.

Please Be Safe!

I wish we lived in a world where this warning was unnecessary! While I don't want to scare you, you need to be aware that over the last few years, nationwide reports of theft and other crime in the real estate sector have increased, particularly at public open houses.

Because of this increase, our national and local associations have instituted major safety education and awareness programs for Realtors®. If you're an unrepresented seller, you're likely to be showing your home to strangers, so please make sure to safeguard your valuables—and *never* show your home alone.

Unrepresented sellers are much more vulnerable to crime because they don't have an agent who can qualify prospects. In fact, one of the greatest values of hiring a professional is to make sure that prospective buyers are, in fact, legitimate. When your home is listed with an agent, it will either be shown by a buyer agent who has a relationship with their buyer-clients, or an unassisted buyer will have to call the listing agent to show the property. The listing agent pre-qualifies the buyer before he ever enters your home.

If you're selling on your own, you need to be particularly diligent in requiring a pre-approval before you let someone into your home. While it's no guarantee, requiring a pre-approval is an important safeguard. Although public open houses are not particularly effective in selling them, they are a popular marketing activity for unrepresented sellers. They carry a much greater risk because, unlike private showings, you can't qualify people before they walk in. Your home is "open" to the public and anyone can come into your home. The homeowner is at great risk for theft immediately, or, more likely later, after being cased. Homeowners alone also risk a personal attack.

When my team is asked to hold a public open house (and we can't talk the seller out of it), we always do it in pairs. Two of us can better keep an eye on the visitors as well as each other.

I'll say it again—if you're trying to sell your home on your own, you need to be cautious. Whether showing your home by appointment or particularly when holding an open house please be safe and never invite strangers into your home when you're by yourself.

PART 2

How About Some Choices?

Why a Real Estate Consultant May be the Best Path

How It Differs From the Traditional Sales Approach

LET'S LOOK AT AN ANALOGY:

The Clothing Store Versus Your Own Personal Shopper

Suppose you had an upcoming trip next month and needed to buy a couple of suits. You have two choices: shop at a leading clothing store or hire a personal shopper.

If you go to the clothing store, the salesperson will probably do his best to sell you a suit from the (limited) inventory in his store. Of course, since he works for the store, his focus is on moving that store's merchandise. If he can please you at the same time, it's a bonus.

The salesperson is working solely on commission; therefore, he only gets paid if you buy a suit right then and there. If you have unique sizing needs and none of the suits at that store fit you properly, the salesperson has no motivation to tell you to go somewhere else. He also may not tell you that a suit you do love is going on sale next week. After all, if you come back in a week, he might not be working that shift. The salesperson may still be ethical. But he's paid to make a sale for the store, not to find the best suits for you.

However, a personal shopper is paid by you to find you the best suits for your needs. Because no two clients are alike, your shopper is going to spend a lot of time upfront really listening and taking note of your lifestyle, career, timetable, size, and price range. Once the shopper does a thorough analysis of your needs, she may recommend one or two particular stores to get you the right suits —when you need them and within your budget.

The personal shopper knows the marketplace and the inventory, so your shopper might tell you not to buy your chosen suit right now because they will be going on sale next week. You harness her expertise to find what is best for you. Your shopper is focused on building a long-term relationship with you, not just putting together a fast transaction.

How will you pay your personal shopper?

- ☞ You can pay by the hour
- ☞ You can pay a flat fee to do a variety of shopping tasks or
- ☞ You can make the pay contingent on your shopper finding you the suits that meet your approval—but you would pay a premium for this choice, because your shopper risks not getting paid.

The same dynamics are at work in real estate consulting.

Consulting in the Real Estate Industry

What exactly IS real estate consulting? It's providing valuable, expert advice to buyers and sellers who need it. While it can include limited service, flat fees, fee-for-service, or commissions, it doesn't adhere to any particular payment method.

True consulting is not a gimmick. And it's not simply a title that an agent puts on her business card because it sounds better.

At its heart, consulting is about offering clear choices, both in the types of services that you can receive and how those services can be paid for.

A true consultant is trained to provide a thorough needs analysis and then offer responsible options to address those needs.

How does it compare to traditional real estate sales? How does it play out in the real world? I will compare some differences between a salesperson and a consultant below.

- ✦ The real estate consultant is compensated for her expertise, time, and/or execution of the task. If she's paid contingent on a guaranteed outcome (the traditional commission), the consumer understands he they will pay a premium for this guarantee.

- ✦ *The real estate salesperson is only paid if and when the house sells.*

- ✦ Like CPAs and most non-personal-injury attorneys, the consultant is retained and is often compensated for time spent and/or services rendered.

✦ *The salesperson is compensated solely on commission. (By the way, this does not mean that a consultant cannot offer commissions, if that's what is right for his client and as long as you, the consumer, understand what you're paying for; the essence of consulting is providing choices.)*

✦ Consulting encompasses many skills and can be used to achieve a variety of outcomes.

✦ *Selling has one single focus—selling something.*

✦ Sometimes the best choice for a consumer is to not buy or sell at all, or not right now.

✦ *When there is no transaction, a salesperson has nothing to offer, and therefore has no way to get paid. The consultant is retained and paid to provide astute counsel to help his client to reach the right decision, based on your individual needs, no matter what the ultimate decision or outcome.*

✦ True consultants believe that they should first understand your needs and goals before suggesting options and solutions. High-pressure selling tactics have no place in the process of providing objective fiduciary counsel.

✦ Once you have objective information about the buying or selling process and what it entails, the consultant must believe wholeheartedly that you, the consumer, are in charge. The consultant can then decide if there is a good fit between your needs and his services.

✦ If the client decides to sell or buy a home, the real estate salesperson has only one way of being paid: a contingent-on-a-sale-commission (the traditional method). Consultants, on the other hand, can offer a variety of compensation alternatives such as an hourly rate or a flat fee for a bundle of services, as well as the traditional commission structure; they can tailor their services based on what you need to reach your goals.

Who Should Hire a Consultant?

In the traditional sales model, we usually think about obtaining real estate services only when we've already made the decision to buy or sell. But in the consultative model, real estate services and counsel are not limited to just transactions and can actually help you evaluate your other choices (such as remodel or wait for a better market) and make an informed decision.

As an example, wouldn't it be great to be able to receive (and pay for) a few hours of objective counsel on expected trends in the real estate market when you're not sure what you want to do?

So, who might be interested in working with a real estate consultant?

- ☞ Any homeowner trying to decide whether to "move or improve."
- ☞ Any home buyer who isn't sure he's ready to buy, but would like some guidance on the current market and the buying process.
- ☞ Any consumer who really doesn't want to play Realtor®, yet feels forced to go it alone to save money.
- ☞ Any consumer who has ever resorted to buying cheap, shoddy services in order to save money and found out too late that she got services that didn't get the job done or didn't get it done right.

FROM THE CONSULTING TIMES:
Excerpted and Adapted from Beware of the Elephants

By ACRE® Ron Stuart

I ATTENDED A SEMINAR ON PROFESSIONALISM IN REAL ESTATE, presented by Bob Wallace, Executive Officer of The Real Estate Board of Greater Vancouver, Canada—and I'd like to share some insights from that seminar that might be useful the next time you want to buy or sell a piece of property .

To be counted as a profession and not just a business, a career must include the following:

✦ The work provides personal service beyond a simple exchange of goods for money.

✦ An independent society maintains standards of ethics, competence, and client satisfaction, including a code of conduct designed to protect the public—and enforced by the society.

✦ Practitioners make a continual investment in improving their skills and knowledge.

As a real estate consumer with property to buy or sell, you want to hire:

1. Someone you can trust,
2. A professional whose specialized knowledge and skill provides more value than you pay out in fees

One great line I can't leave out: "...just doing it and getting paid sounds more like prostitution than professionalism."

But for the most part, today's real estate world is only an industry, and not a profession. Here's where I see a disconnect: we are sworn to act only in the best interests of our clients, but we get paid only when we close a sale. Thus, we Realtors® face tremendous pressure to act in our own self interest and close the deal, whether or not it's really the right thing for our client. We get training and education in our fiduciary obligation to our clients—only to return afterward to the office, where selling reigns supreme. Thus, the dichotomy. *Professionals advise and serve in the client's best interest — salespeople sell!*

Regrettably, success in our industry is measured by sales productivity, not by fiduciary integrity. MLS® Awards reward sales success. Qualification for reward trips and other perks are measured by sales. Offices have regular "sales meetings." Our "SOLD" signs hanging on clients' lawns trumpet our sales prowess. Individual marketing material implies that I can sell your property better than another agent can. But as a client, you don't need to be sold; you need to receive advocacy and be advised, represented, coached and guided.

If selling is persuading another to buy something we wish to sell, and professionalism is providing valuable services for a fee, I have to wonder whether there can be such a thing as "professional sales."

Can a sales culture and a culture of true professionalism co-exist? Can the former be re-morphed into the latter? Does the leopard change its spots? Consumers have always seen us as salespeople; they are well aware that commission is the life blood of our existence. Yet we have the audacity to inform clients that we will place their interests above all others, including our own. Whom do we think we're kidding?

Bringing our industry to a point where it truly does "walk the talk" is no small undertaking. I commend ACRE® for your initiative.

How Fees and Hourly Compensation Work

You Can Save Money Without Being Discounted

BY NOW, YOU UNDERSTAND that quality real estate representation is essential for keeping the most money in your pocket when you close and that you don't have to be locked into paying by commission in order to get that quality!

Of course, after you've explored and weighed different options, based on your individual needs and comfort level, you may find—as many consumers do—that a traditional commission is the best choice for you. And that's perfectly fine. You should make that choice because it's the best option for you, not because it's the only option.

Before we review some of the different compensation possibilities, let's look at what is involved when you pay for real estate consulting services by the hour or by a flat fee.

Obtaining Real Estate Services by Fee or by the Hour

When you pay for real estate services, either by a flat fee or by the hour, you can often (but not always) save a lot of money. But unlike using a discount agent who agrees to cut her commission, you don't have to sacrifice the number or the quality of the services you receive. By choosing a flat fee for a bundle of services, or paying by the hour, you receive and pay for only the services or time received. You are not receiving a guaranteed outcome, but you also do not have to pay a premium for that guarantee—the "insurance" that if you don't achieve the desired outcome, you pay nothing. That's what makes the savings possible.

Actually, paying for services by fee or by the hour isn't that radical an idea. Consider that most professionals and service providers are paid via fees or hourly rates, and for good reason. Let's take a look at a few examples:

+ A couple wants to start a family, but after months of trying, they are not able to conceive. After getting a referral from the wife's doctor, they make an appointment with a fertility specialist. The couple has some tests run, and after conferring with the physician, they confirm that the wife is a candidate for in-vitro fertilization.

The physician or nurse-practitioner then reviews the entire procedure with the couple as well as how the clinic will be paid—usually a flat fee for a certain number of tries. Is there a risk on the part of that couple in paying in this way? Absolutely! Because even though the clinic is highly recommended, the couple could spend thousands of dollars without achieving a successful pregnancy. The clinic can influence, but certainly not control, the outcome. *The clinic and the specialists are paid for the services rendered, whether or not the couple achieves a successful pregnancy.*

+ A businessman is quickly climbing the corporate ladder. But with the constant changes in the tax code, his taxes are getting more and more complicated, and preparing them each year is very time consuming. The businessman thinks that he could save a lot of money in deductions if he hires a professional Certified Public Accountant (CPA) to prepare his taxes.

The following week, he brings all his work stubs and receipts to a CPA who comes highly recommended by a friend. The CPA looks all the paperwork over and tells the businessman that she charges X$ per hour, and the taxes will take approximately X hours to prepare. Is there a risk on the part of the businessman in paying the CPA by the hour? Absolutely, because even though the CPA is skilled, she cannot control the outcome—the businessman could end up saving money or he could end up paying more in taxes. *The CPA is being paid for her services, time, and expertise, regardless of what the businessman ends up paying in taxes.*

+ A homeowner hires a painter to remove old wallpaper and then to paint her living room. The painter quotes the estimated material costs, his hourly rate, and the expected number of hours it will take to complete the job, and the owner hires him.

The painter gets started, but soon finds there are three additional layers of wallpaper underneath the visible one. In order to do the job, it will now take the painter many hours more than what was originally estimated. Did the homeowner take a risk hiring the painter by the hour plus materials? Of course, because clearly, the painter can't control the unexpected obstacle, and even though the homeowner could stop the work if she could not afford the additional cost, she'd still have to pay the painter for the work already completed. *The painter is being paid for the materials purchased and the work already done, regardless of the discovery of the additional necessary work.*

Real estate professionals have traditionally been paid contingent on an outcome, even though—like the clinic, the CPA, and the painter in the previous examples—no matter how skilled they are, they cannot control that outcome. The initial pricing of a home and the economic climate will determine how fast and for how much a home sells for. To illustrate, let's take a look at a couple of opposite real estate markets:

When I was writing the original edition of this book, my local market was experiencing a rapid shift from a crazy "seller's market" to a "buyer's market." The seller's market that we experienced for five to seven years was characterized by a shortage of available homes and historically low interest rates that greatly increased the pool of interested buyers. During this time, it was not uncommon for a home to come on the market and within a few hours, have multiple offers. Prices escalated quickly and "days on market" were on average, extremely low. Investors were buying homes, reselling them within a year, and reaping huge profits. Homeowners could sell their own homes fairly easily, even if they were not skilled in marketing and negotiations. As long as they could stick a sign in the yard, they could sell their home and even turn a tidy profit.

Yet, even during this seller's market, the skill of an agent was still a big asset, particularly with buyers. An experienced buyer agent could often, in a multiple bid situation, "tip the scales" toward their buyer by structuring an offer to favor the seller, when all the offering prices were close.

As an example, I worked with a couple during this time who beat out the other buyers for the home they wanted even though they could not compete on price—the house was listed for $350,000 and they could only go up to $345,000. My clients got the house because they followed my advice and offered terms that favored the seller. This is where an agent whose practice involves representing both buyers and sellers has a distinct advantage over those who are exclusively listing or buyer agents. I knew from my experience as a listing agent that taking a house off the market for a long period of time was a big concern for many sellers. So, in the offer to purchase we agreed that if the seller accepted this offer, the home inspection would be completed within 48 hours. And since my buyers couldn't compete on price, you'd better believe that I included a warm and fuzzy cover letter to the sellers pointing out that my buyers did not have a house to sell, they could put 10 percent (versus 5 percent) down, and that they would close whenever the seller wanted to.

As much as my experience and expertise could influence the outcome for my buyers, I certainly could not control it. I had no power over a market that offered five buyers for every home and sometimes produced bidding wars that my buyer-clients would lose. Many of my buyers during this time had to settle for a home that was less than what they wanted because there was such a great shortage of homes. *Again, while I could use my skills to influence the outcome, I could not control it.*

Fast-forward a few years to 2007, where my local market had becoming a buyer's market. In this environment, the experience and expertise of an agent was particularly needed on the listing (seller's) side. During a seller's market, all that needed to be done to sell a home was list it in the MLS and put a sign in the yard. But selling a home in a buyer's market is a different story. A buyer's market is characterized by an abundance of available homes—often with five homes for every available buyer. There are far fewer buyers looking. The days on market rapidly increase as inventory swells. Buyers can take their time, going back to see possibilities three and four times. Prices decline and buyers can negotiate a great deal.

In a buyer's market, the skills of a listing agent can be very important in influencing whether her listing sells before the competition. It is no longer enough to rely on a sign or the MLS; now the agent's skills, particularly her proficiency in technology and the Internet, become paramount. The visibility of an agent's website and the capability to provide virtual tours, floor plans, and town reports online, where they can be accessed by the greatest number of potential buyers, can make a big difference. In this type of buyer's market, the agent's skills in interpreting the environment and monitoring what is and isn't selling, as well as communicating with the seller in a timely manner on matters of pricing, become absolutely critical in influencing whether or not the home sells.

Again, as much as a listing agent's skills and proficiency can influence the results for a seller, the agent cannot control the outcome. The listing agent has no power over the number of homes on the market greatly exceeding the number of available buyers. The agent cannot control the fact that prices are falling due to this imbalance. In this market, the agent's ability to communicate honestly and with empathy with her seller is imperative—because selling a home in this market comes down, ultimately, to price. Experienced agents know that every home will sell for the right price. But we also know that no amount of marketing will sell an overpriced home. *In other words, a listing agent can influence the outcome but not control it.*

> With the current traditional commission system, agents are paid as though they could control the outcome—and that "insurance policy" of only paying if the house sells makes this method of compensation very expensive to the consumer.

Risk Versus Reward

When I explain to a potential client how he can save a lot of money by paying for an agent's time or services of, rather than the outcome, he often responds, *"What if the agent doesn't do a good job?"* But by that reasoning, you would have to question whether any service provider whose pay was not contingent on the outcome would do a good job .

As an example, a dentist is paid for his services and expertise, regardless of what dental issues come up. No matter how skilled the dentist is, he cannot control whether you only need twice-a-year cleanings or an abundance of root canals, bridges or implants. He might influence your future dental health by making care suggestions, but he certainly cannot control what ultimately happens with your mouth—that depends on hereditary factors and how diligently you care for your teeth. If the dentist is paid for his services regardless of what comes up, how do you know that he will do a good job? You have no guarantee! That's why you usually don't pick a dentist from the phone book; it's far better to get a referral from a happy patient.

School teachers are paid a salary regardless of how many of their students ace the SATs. They are paid, and promoted, based on their teaching skills, not necessarily by how many students go on to college.

And so it is with most service providers. Obviously, if you pay for someone's services by non-contingent fee or by the hour, you need to have confidence that the provider will do quality work. Although some consumers believe that a real estate agent will work harder knowing that she will only be paid if the house sells, the reality is that top-notch Realtors®, like any other good service provider, work hard for their clients because they want to safeguard their reputation for quality work, and because they want to continue earning referrals.

Smart consumers seeking any service provider ask for a referral from someone they know or, ask the prospective provider for references. If they find that the provider has done a good job for other customers, clients, or patients, there is a very good chance that he'll do a good job for you, no matter how he's paid.

Inside Tip: Choosing an Agent

When I speak with consumers who were disappointed with their last real estate agent, I first ask how they chose that agent. Nine times out of ten, they chose them based on advertising rather than by referral. I find this curious because we usually choose other service providers by asking someone we trust for a referral.

For instance, most women would *never* choose their hairdresser from a list on the Internet or from a magazine ad. Their hair is too important to them. So they ask a couple of friends, whose haircuts they like, where they go.

Would you want to put your child's health into the hands of a pediatrician based on a lot of ads in the yellow pages saying how good they are?

How about a mechanic? Would you want to hire someone to service your car based solely on a lot of ads saying, "trust me"?

Yet some people will put their largest financial investment in the hands of a stranger whose only credential is that they dropped a whole lot of money into putting their face (along with the claim that they are #1) on billboards, park benches, and shopping carts.

The best way to choose an agent is not by the production numbers they claim or the amount of advertising they do. Rather, get a referral from someone you trust. Find a friend or co-worker who has recently sold her home and ask if he'd recommend his agent. Good, reputable agents get the majority of their business primarily by referral. Period.

Now, I want to be very clear: Paying for real estate services by non-contingent fees is not for everyone! As my mom likes to say, "That's why they make chocolate and vanilla." Some people are risk-averse; particularly if they are working with an agent that they know and trust, they may be better off paying a traditional commission. There's nothing wrong with that as long as they understand that they are paying a premium to eliminate risk. But a growing number of folks, once they understand that the outcome is not controlled by the agent, would rather forego the guarantee and pay less by fee, while still getting quality services and counsel.

Financial Services as a Model for Real Estate

When we designed the ACRE® Program for real estate professionals, we looked at the financial industry as an example of how an industry can evolve from being salespeople paid by commission to consultants paid largely by fee.

In the early 1980's, "financial planners" were, for the most part, stockbrokers and other salespeople who provided "free" consultations and made their money by selling financial products. Like real estate salespeople today that call themselves "consultants" because it sounds better, financial salespeople then would often call themselves "financial planners."

However, as the 1980's wore on, consumers who wanted truly objective advice (and were willing to pay for it) demanded a choice, and from this consumer demand, the CFP® (Certified Financial Planner) was born.

Now, despite the tremendous increase in CFPs® over the last two decades, there are still plenty of commission-only financial salespeople. But there's a clear line of demarcation between financial salespeople who are paid to sell products, and CFP®'s who are paid to provide objective counsel and guidance to their clients.

There will probably always be a niche for real estate salespeople whose primary job is moving the inventory. However, we believe more and more consumers will demand professional real estate consultants whose primary job is not to move the product, but rather to act as an advisor and advocate for their clients.

How About Some Choices?
(Yes, One of Them Is Traditional Commissions)

IN THE FIFTEEN YEARS I've spent developing compensation alternatives in real estate, I've wondered why agents are still overwhelmingly paid by commission, when the public can benefit hugely by having choices. And the benefits are not just financial. Consider some common scenarios:

+ You are thinking of doing some remodeling and wonder what improvements will get you the most money when you are ready to sell. You would clearly benefit from an agent's knowledge of your neighborhood and town—*before* plunking down a bunch of money. But the traditional commission system won't help because it only pays the agent for a sale, not a consultation.

As long as you are limited to two choices—commissions or nothing—you either call in someone you don't know and question the objectivity of her advice (especially if she thinks there's potential for a listing), or you see if you can find an agent friend who will counsel you for free. Most consumers simply "wing it," based on their limited knowledge, and hope for the best.

+ Your tax bill seems to be increasing every year. You wonder if your town's assessment of your home is off, but with a full-time job, you have no time to research this? A Realtor® could certainly check, if there was a way you could compensate him for his time.

+ While the interest rates are relatively low, you'd like to refinance—*if* you have enough equity in your home. To determine this before you spend money and time on a refinance, you need to know your home's current value. Wouldn't it be great if you could pay a Realtor® a reasonable flat fee to complete a comparative market analysis (CMA) and review it with you?

✦ You're thinking about buying your first home, but you're not sure if you can afford a home t meets your requirements. If you meet with an agent, you are concerned that she won't give you objective advice because she's only paid if you buy. But wouldn't it be great if you could meet with a consultant, especially if she would credit all or part of her fee, if and when you later decide to purchase a home through her?

✦ You've outgrown your home (or your house has outgrown you), and you're facing the "move or improve" decision. Can you trust an agent to be objective about this decision, when he only gets paid for his time and effort if you sell? But what if you could meet with a trained consultant and pay for truly objective advice?

There are more examples, but you get the idea. Clearly, it makes sense to have alternatives. The legal profession offers a great model of choice:

✦ Many areas of law, such as providing advice on a tricky legal problem, lend themselves to hourly compensation.

✦ Some areas, such as real estate law, are usually paid with a flat fee for a task or a group of tasks.

✦ And high-risk specialties, such as personal injury, are almost always paid on contingency (with an enormous payoff for success).

Can we have the same choices in real estate? You bet! There is nothing written in stone that says that real estate services have to be paid by commission and commission only. Ask any real estate manager why her agents are paid by commission and you'll usually hear, "That's the way we've always done it."

ACRE® Coach Merv Forney sums it up:

The real estate industry is very resistant to change, and it is a "me too" industry with a million Realtors® all doing the same thing. In my real estate practice, I decided that to compete in this arena and to seek out my client's common interests, I would have a different value proposition to offer consumers.

When looking at the three choices—an hourly rate, a flat fee, or a traditional commission—there is no right or wrong choice. As in the legal profession, different choices work in different scenarios. It's the same in real estate, where consumers have different needs and comfort levels.

Merv continues,

> *Based on an NAR study done back in 2000, they predicted that consulting was going to be the wave of the future. The truth is one size does not fit all, which is why in my practice, we offered three choices to our clients: traditional (percentage) commission, a fee-for-service schedule, and an hourly rate.*

Currently, real estate consulting is in its nascent stage, yet is growing ever more popular for the consumer. Based on this demand, the Accredited Consultant in Real Estate (ACRE®) Course and Coaching Program was launched in 2006 to train real estate professionals as consultants. ACRE® is committed to developing a large pool of skilled real estate consultants who are willing to work with you to provide the advice you need, while avoiding the expensive and often-inappropriate full-commission model unless that makes sense for you. If you'd like to work with a knowledgeable, certified consultant trained to meet *your* needs and not some arbitrary ancient policies, check out the ACRE® Locator at www.TheConsultingTimes.com/find to find an ACRE® near you.

If there isn't an ACRE® in your area, don't be afraid to seek out good agents and ask if they (and their brokers) would be willing to consider different compensation. Many agents are not aware of real estate consulting and have never thought about doing real estate this way. If they seem interested, but need information, give them this book to read, send them to our consulting site, www.TheConsultingTimes.com, or have them watch the videos at www.ACREonYouTube.com. The marketplace and environment have shown that as time moves on, more agents will be either trained in the consulting model or at least open to learning this new approach.

Some Payment Options to Consider

1. **An hourly rate capped at a set number of hours:** This option helps the consumer who would like to sit down and get some professional counsel. It's also good for buyers who would prefer to pay their buyer agent themselves and have the money go toward the offered co-broke on the house they decide to buy.

   My favorite application of hourly compensation is for sellers who find their own buyer. Some sellers I have worked with had actually run ads, shown their own home, and found a buyer who wanted to write up an offer. If the buyer also did not have representation, it was "the blind leading the blind." This is when many sellers would say to me, "OK, I've found my buyer, but I have no earthly idea of what to do next." Or, sometimes the seller found a buyer who was represented—and faced trying to negotiate against a pro who does it all the time.

   Over the years, I've worked with sellers who found buyers by happenstance prior to even marketing their home. They might have mentioned at work that they were thinking of selling their home, and someone said, "Hey, I've seen your home—I would like to buy it." Sometimes, it's a friend or a family member who wants to buy it. In these cases, a small payment to a Realtor® can save you a ton of cash. This option makes a lot of sense for sellers who have procured their own buyer and need the agent to negotiate. More importantly, a consultant can ensure that the seller is not taken to the cleaners, that there are no surprises, and that the house closes on schedule.

   To give you an idea of the savings, let's say the real estate consultant charges $150 per hour, and the cap is at six hours (this is our average to negotiate and troubleshoot a transaction). If it takes six hours, you would pay the consultant $900. Compare that to a commission, even a discounted commission, and you can see the savings. For $900, you receive the most important services that you can get from a skilled agent—negotiating and troubleshooting—and you have kept yourself protected. Compare this to a discounted commission that "covers" all tasks (including marketing tasks, which you don't need), but waters down the quality. This is a situation where a commission, like a round peg going into a square hole, simply doesn't fit the seller's needs, but the hourly rate is perfect!

2. **À la carte services.** Many consultants, including my team, offer functionary marketing services and materials à la carte. Examples include digital photography, floor plan, feature packages, or a demographic report of the town to give potential buyers. While you can certainly do these things yourself, a full-time agent has the equipment, tools, and know-how to do them better and faster, and it's usually worth the cost.

   One very important à la carte service that you should consider asking an agent to provide is exposure of your home on her website. Many agents are willing and able to put your home on their site with the understanding that if they procure a buyer for you, you'll pay their buyer-side fee. Internet presence is extremely important, especially if you are not listed on the MLS, and this is one area that sellers can't easily replicate themselves. For this, you want an agent who is not only willing, but one whose website is ranked high in the search engines, to provide maximum exposure.

   Important! Purchasing à la carte services should be limited to functionary tasks and services!

   As we discussed earlier, limited service like MLS Entry Only is usually a disaster for sellers. If you want to be on the MLS, make sure that you bundle your listing with the negotiating and troubleshooting services of a pro.

3. **Flat-fee for a bundle of services.** Unfortunately, flat fees have long been associated with limited services, primarily MLS Entry Only, which has been overwhelmingly unsuccessful for sellers. This is a shame because a flat fee, if structured to include vital fiduciary services, is a fabulous option

for sellers who don't need the insurance of a contingent-on-the-sale commission.

And flat-fee packages can be very simple. An example of a basic package includes a thorough, up-to-date CMA, assistance completing all forms, a sign and/or lockbox, entry into the MLS, and—this is vital—negotiating and troubleshooting the transaction. In other words, the seller takes on most functionary tasks and marketing, while paying the agent to step in and do what he does best—getting the most money for the property and troubleshooting the transaction so that it closes on time.

Flat-fee packages can also be very elaborate and include everything that a seller would typically get with a commission, except the insurance policy. My team's experience with sellers who prefer to pay a non-contingent flat fee rather than a commission is that eight out of ten want full service. They don't have the time or the desire to "play Realtor®." But they want to forego the high cost of paying for an outcome rather than the services themselves.

Interestingly, on average, those sellers who chose my agency's full service package realized a higher sales price for their home, and their home's market time was noticeably decreased. We believe this is because both our full-service fee and full-service commission packages provide a full compliment of cutting-edge marketing, both online and off; this marketing attracts more prospects, and thus, better results.

Yet there are plenty of ways to construct packages that strike a middle ground—all fiduciary services plus limited functionary and marketing. The choices are only limited by what works for both you and your consultant.

The fees for various packages will vary from market to market and consultant to consultant. In our ACRE® program, we teach agents how to determine their hourly rates; better agents will charge more, but will usually be worth the added cost because of what they save their clients. We also guide them in developing various flat-fee packages by determining how many hours it takes to complete various tasks, adding in material costs and a fair and reasonable profit. It is often an eye-opener to agents, who, for the first time, are coming face-to-face with their actual costs of doing business.

4. **Traditional commission**. Any discussion of choices must include the traditional commission option.

First of all, there are certain circumstances where paying by commission makes sense. For instance, if you are not 100 percent sure that you must sell your home, no matter what price you get, paying a non-contingent fee won't necessarily work for you. Or if you are selling a condo or a lower priced home, you may find that you actually pay less by commission. This is because the costs associated with various tasks remain the same, whether they are done to market a $50,000 condo or a $500,000 home. We have found in our market that under a certain sales price, the seller actually pays less when paying by commission.

Second, some folks are financially conservative by nature. That's fine. Choices are all about the freedom to have alternatives. On an intellectual level, some folks may understand that the agent cannot control the outcome, but they would still prefer that the agent take the risk. If that is you, there is nothing wrong with paying by commission— as long as you understand that you will be paying more to have that "safety net."

When Paula Bean speaks to clients, she states the simple truth:

I'm not a regular real estate agent. I'm an Accredited Consultant in Real Estate (ACRE®). My job is to ask you some questions to see what you are trying to accomplish so I can determine your needs, wants, and time frame. I can recommend what I think is best for you, and then, what you do is up to you. You can have no risk and do traditional commission, but with commissions the less you pay them, the less quality you are going to get, it's that simple.

Choices: what you do is up to you.

Determining What You Need

THE VERY ESSENCE OF REAL ESTATE CONSULTING is giving you, the consumer, choices. But in order to make the best choices, you have to honestly evaluate your needs, capabilities, and the time that you're able and willing to devote to the task of buying or selling your home.

Good news! The ACRE® program has developed Seller and Buyer Needs Analyses that do just that. In a few minutes, in the privacy of your home or office, you can review the various tasks involved in selling or buying a home, determine which ones make sense to do yourself, which ones you might like a pro to handle, and which ones you can skip entirely.

Many consumers have told us that completing the analysis was the best thing they did in the selling or buying process. This analysis will help you to determine where your needs may lie, confident that tasks or expertise that you might not have thought about won't sneak up and bite you later in the process. And if you find that you need professional assistance, we'll help you to get the most bang for your buck.

Whether you are toying with the idea of trying to sell on your own, bringing in a pro for some services, hiring someone for the whole enchilada, or simply need an hour or so of counsel, it is important to proceed with your eyes open.

I must stress again the importance of being an educated consumer before you start spending money. Real estate can look deceptively easy until you are knee-deep in the time-sensitive morass of requirements and obligations.

Paula Bean explains to her clients:

> My job is to educate. Most people think there are two or three things
> to do when selling a home, like you either show the house or put a

sign in the yard, and then you wait for people to come and say, "I want to buy it." But the first question I always ask when working with a new client is, "Why are you selling?" because everything that follows is based on their answer.

A Promise You Can Take To The Bank

While I can't speak for all real estate agents, I can tell you that if you're working with an ACRE®, if we honestly feel that you can do just fine without our services, we're going to tell you so. Many times, ACRE®s have met with would-be sellers who we truly felt would be better off not selling at that time or not selling at all and we've told them just that. One thing ACRE®s want you to know: we have absolutely no interest in wasting your money or time (there are plenty of outfits that do that). As accredited consultants, we have a reputation for honesty, straight talk, and ethics—and that reputation is far more important to us than a few bucks from someone who doesn't need to spend them.

We're also going to tell you if we can't accommodate what you want. Sadly, many agents will do almost anything, and work with almost anyone. We only work with you if we truly feel that our services are a good match with your needs.

In real estate, there's Nordstrom and there's Walmart. There's nothing wrong with Walmart if what you're buying is a commodity...a product that's the same. But we believe that quality real estate services are NOT a commodity; therefore, we only provide Nordstrom. Now, we will offer different ways to pay for Nordstrom, but in terms of the services we provide, we will only do Nordstrom because quality is what brings you the most money in your pocket when you walk away from the closing table, and Nordstrom is what we, as consultants, will put our names to. Now, there are some consumers that may want Walmart. And if you're one of those consumers there are tons of Walmart agents out there. But that's not what we do.

It's not what you save...it's what you keep! As is true in other fiduciary fields, quality real estate services and counsel will always provide you the best value, even after subtracting the commission or fee. Shoddy, discount services are a waste of your money, no matter how cheap they are. In determining your needs, we provide real estate CHOICE—and it WON'T be shoddy!

Why Choose an Accredited Consultant in Real Estate (ACRE)®?

REAL ESTATE PROFESSIONALS who have earned the ACRE® certification have completed a course of study and taken an exam that tests their ability to provide unbiased counsel to the consumer in matters that deal with real estate. The program provides them the tools to offer different choices to the consumer based on a comprehensive needs analysis. In addition, most ACREs® continue increasing their knowledge and skills, and staying current with market shifts and trends, through the Graduate Coaching Exchange.

Accredited Consultants in Real Estate® consult WITH their clients, rather than sell TO them. So, rather than hiring a salesperson whose sole focus tends to be "making the sale," a consultant helps you attain your goals, which may or may not involve a sale.

But because, under the traditional commission model, a Realtor® is only paid if a sale takes place, consumers often turn to attorneys to negotiate offers and troubleshoot their transactions. Unfortunately, most attorneys don't work day-to-day in the real estate market—so they're not the best choice either to hammer out the best deal and or to stay on top of the numerous details of a successful and completed transaction.

Instead, you can hire an ACRE® to do just the tasks you need done—*and* provide that crucial expertise. At last, you can pay for advice, counsel, and experience from the professional who knows the most about real estate. If you want to buy or sell, or are facing a decision to "move or improve," you can pay for those particular services only, and at the same time, receive unbiased advice and counsel.

My colleague, Paula Bean, discussed the benefit of expert help in answering the "improve or move" question in an article for The Consulting Times. I'll excerpt it here:

To move or improve your home? You'd like help to decide, without be-ing pressured into listing your home for sale. That means seeking out unbiased help from someone who's not trying to get your signature on a contract and a sign in your yard. You need an experienced real estate consultant who will be able to help you make a good decision both now (to move or not?) and in the future (if you do stay, not over-improving your house).

The hardest time we have in selling houses is when someone has over-improved the home and they can't get the price they need when they do sell, in order to buy the next property they want. These often become "expired" rather than "sold" listings. Because of the over-im-provement, sellers lose money and are sometimes driven to try selling without professional help so they can avoid paying a commission, but this strategy frequently doesn't work. Statistics show that professional counsel virtually always saves you money (and time too).

I recently had a consumer call me for this very reason. He was think-ing of retiring in 3 or 4 years, but wanted to make some improvements to the home in the meantime. He didn't want to be pressured to sell, he just wanted to know if the renovations he and his wife had in mind would give him a return when he did sell. He had several agents who lived in his subdivision as well, so I asked him why he called me for consulting when he could get it free from anyone. He said "because I just need unbiased advice, I don't want to sell right now and I don't want someone to do it free, I want an unbiased expert opinion and nothing is free. For a competent opinion, you need to pay for it." (by the way, he was a CPA and said he wouldn't do somebody's taxes free and wondered why agents work for free).

When you need an experienced professional to handle the fiduciary responsibilities of a home sale, such as qualifying the buyer, dealing with various disclosures, and/or supporting you in the negotiations, you can now obtain these vital services from an ACRE®, through an hourly fee or package price, without having to complete a transaction or pay a com-mission.

The bottom line is that the essence of real estate consulting is the ability to provide you with informed, current-market choices—and that's exactly what ACRE®-certified consultants do. For the consumer, whether you pay an ACRE® for a few hours of consultation, a flat fee for a bundle of services, or choose to pay in the traditional commission structure, you will now receive and pay for only the services that fit your current needs and comfort level.

To find an ACRE® near you, check out the ACRE® Locator at: www.TheConsultingTimes/find.

PART 3

The Four Financial Potholes

Pricing Your Home to Sell for the Highest Value

IF YOU WISH TO GET TOP DOLLAR for your home and a quick sale, let's look at the three big questions we get from consumers regarding pricing:

1. "What price can I get?"
2. "How long will it take?"
3. "Who determines price anyway?"

In other words..."*I need the straight scoop on pricing!*"

There is a big difference between a listing price, which the seller determines, and a selling price, which is controlled by the market. Or to put it another way, the seller sets the price— but ultimately, the buyer determines the value. In addition, there are certain things that do and do not affect value.

In fact, here's one of the hardest concepts for consumers to grasp: what you spend to acquire, fix up, or maintain a home has much less bearing on how much you can sell it for than you might think. The real question is how it stacks up against homes of similar size, location, and quality in today's current market. If you're thinking about improving your home and want to know if you'll be able to recapture the cost of the improvement when you sell, expert advice can make a big difference.

Another place where expert advice can really make a difference is in setting the asking price. It goes against common sense, but setting a price that's either too high *or* too low can undermine the sales process and vacuum thousands of dollars right out of your wallet. We'll explore why in a moment. But first, we need to examine some of the factors that do or don't make a difference in the price your home will command.

Things That Don't Affect Value

✦ **Your original cost.** One of the things that buyers consistently ask when they are interested in a home is, "What did the seller pay when they bought the house?" as though that would be a factor in what they should offer. The answer is, it doesn't matter! You may have paid top dollar to buy your home few years back in a seller's market when prices were sky-high. You may have scored a great deal because you bought in a buyer's market. But what you paid when you bought has absolutely no bearing on what you can ask today.

✦ **The cost to rebuild today.** Building costs will go up and they will go down. They have nothing to do with market value.

✦ **Money spent on certain not-the-best-for-resale improvements.** There is a mantra that I constantly repeat to would-be sellers, "What you put into your home is not necessarily what you will get out of it." Remodeling a bath will return 102 percent of your investment, but building a home office will only get you 72 percent back. (Source: NAR 2005 Cost vs. Value Report) It doesn't mean that you shouldn't make your home what you want—there is something to be said for personal enjoyment. But don't expect an automatic dollar-for-dollar return. It doesn't work that way.

✦ **Personal attachment.** That huge built-in shelving unit that takes up half of your living room may hold many memories for you because of what it showcased through the years, but has no bearing on its value to a potential buyer.

Things That Do Affect Value

✦ **Market value.** The price that will bring a sale between a willing buyer and a willing seller. It is based on the history of similar properties recently sold in the area.

✦ **Regression and progression:** The effect that surrounding home sizes have on the value of a subject property.

Regression is the decrease in value of a more expensive home when surrounded by smaller homes. For example, a homeowner may have added a second story to his ranch-style home years ago to accommodate his large family. However, if all of the other homes on his street have remained one-story ranches, his two-story would lose value.

✦ *Progression* is the increase in value of a less expensive home when surrounded by larger homes. For example, if a neighborhood of small homes all expanded over the years except for one, that smaller home would gain value.

The amenity itself. *Value is determined not by the cost invested in a property, but by the value derived from it.* For example, let's say you have two identical homes and both need a well. House A puts in a well for $9,000. House B hits rock and the cost for that well is $17,000. The market value of both homes would still be the same. The home with the more expensive well is worth no more—because the value is in the water, not the cost of obtaining it.

✦ **Investment in good resale improvements:** The best return on an investment in 2005 was a mid-range bath remodel (102 percent) followed by a minor kitchen remodel (98 percent). (Source: NAR 2005 Cost vs. Value Report)

The Top 10 Most Frequently Heard Pricing Comments from Sellers to Realtors®

Which, truth be told, have no actual bearing on correctly pricing a home. Sorry.

1. "Our home is so much nicer than those other houses."
2. "Well, my cousin, who is an agent, said it was worth a lot more."
3. "People always offer less than asking price."
4. "We can always come down on our price."
5. "We simply have to get that much out of our home."
6. "My neighbor was able to get his price."
7. "We are going to try it at our price for a month or so."
8. "But look at all of the nice upgrades we put in."
9. "The buyers can always make an offer."
10. "We paid more when we bought it."

The Importance of Pricing It Right...

A well-priced listing is the most important factor in marketing your property for the greatest value. Nothing, I repeat, nothing can touch this. Naturally, listing a property too low will leave money on the table. But setting the price too high discourages showings—and actually tends to discourage the most likely buyers from even viewing your property. Setting the price too high, in other words, can backfire, resulting in a damaging need to reduce the price later, and then negotiate down from the reduced price to a lower number than you could have had if you'd price the house accurately to start with.

...From the Beginning!

Pricing your home correctly in the beginning will net you more. Consider these statistics:

Average Difference Between Original List Price and Selling Price by Length of Time on Market*	
2.9%	Less Than 4 Weeks
4.8%	4-12 Weeks
6.4%	13-24 Weeks
9.1%	More Than 24 Weeks
* Based on NAR Home Buying & Selling Survey - 2004	

One of the top 10 pricing comments cited previously is "We are going to try it at our price for a month or so." The problem with this logic is that the longer a home is on the market, the less it will ultimately get. If your home is listed too high in that crucial first couple of weeks, you lose your best opportunity to sell for close to market value.

History of an Overpriced Home

	MONTH 1	MONTH 2	MONTH 3	MONTH 4	MONTH 5	MONTH 6
LIST PRICE: $280,000	🏠					
REDUCED TO: $270,000		🏠				
REDUCED TO: $260,000			🏠			
REDUCED TO: $250,000	ACTUAL MARKET VALUE			🏠		
SOLD AT: $235,000					🏠	🏠

A few years back, a member of my team, Dina Raneri, went on a listing appointment. After carefully reviewing the sales comparables, she recommended a list price to the sellers of $250,000, which was what the market indicated and would probably enable them to sell their home within 30 days. Dina explained that if the home is priced to the market from the beginning, it will usually sell for very close to list and perhaps even more because there was a shortage of homes at $250,000 or less.

The sellers, however, insisted on listing at $280,000. They then began a process of what we call "chasing the market" i.e., dropping the price month in and out to try to get an offer. Unfortunately, by the time an overpriced home is finally reduced to the market value it originally was, it is too "aged" for buyers to offer full price.

Have you ever asked how long a home has been on the market? What conclusions do you draw?

As you can see, in the prior table, Dina's sellers paid dearly for overpricing their home: instead of selling for $250,000 or more in a month of market time, they took six months to sell, and only got $230,000!

"BUT WE HAVE TIME!"

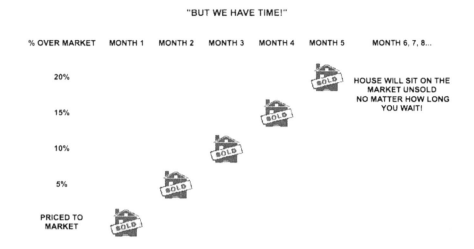

At some percentage above the market, no reasonable amount of time will produce a sale.

"COULDN'T WE TRY IT FOR A COUPLE OF WEEKS?"

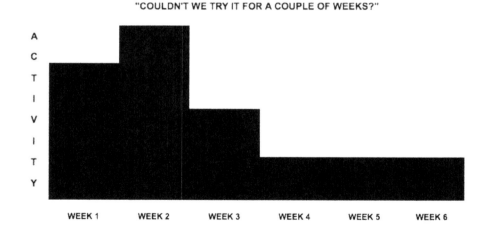

The majority of prospect activity on a new listing occurs in the first two weeks it is on the market. This happens because buyer agents maintain an inventory of active prospects who they've been cultivated over time. When a home is newly listed, agents arrange for buyers to see it. Once this active group has seen the property, showing activity decreases to only those buyers new to the market. For this reason it is very important that sellers have their home in the best condition and at the best price at first exposure to the market.

Overpricing Is a Very Human Thing to Do

It is natural to try to get as much as possible for your property. It is natural to think your home will be the exception to the rule. We all hope that we will find the one buyer who will fall desperately in love with our house and pay our price. It is also natural to reason that you can drop your price later. But while these thoughts are human nature—they simply ignore the realities of the market.

Overpricing...

+ Reduces agent activity

+ Reduces advertising response

+ Loses interested buyers

+ Attracts the wrong prospects

+ Eliminates offers

+ Helps sell the competition

+ Extends market time

+ Causes appraisal problems

When you hire a professional to assist you in selling your home, one of the first and most important things she will do is to prepare an analysis of the market and use her knowledge and expertise to arrive at a probable price range. If you hired her because you trust her judgment, do yourself a favor and *listen*.

Believe me, putting a price on a home is one of the hardest jobs of a listing agent. It's not that the price range is hard to set. The "actives," "under agreements," and "solds"—all crucial to evaluating and understanding the market—are right at our fingertips. Rather it is telling a homeowner, who may have put years of love into her home, that it may not sell for what she thinks it's "worth."

A real estate professional who has a reputation for quality work will be firm and tell you what the market is showing, even if it's not what you want to hear. And by doing so, he takes the risk of losing your listing, even though he's being true and ethical. Unfortunately, many sellers continue the erroneous practice of choosing an agent based on who sets the highest price.

But the *market* determines the selling price for your home, not the agent or the agent's company. The agent's marketing can certainly influence in your favor, but it can *never* control when your home will sell, or for how much.

Marketing is still essential; a listing agent's job is to bring your home to the attention of the greatest number of qualified buyers. Her experience, expertise, and guidance are what will make the difference in your profitability when you walk away from the closing table.

Unfortunately, less ethical agents who are desperate for business will tell consumers whatever price range they think they need to obtain the listing. In the business, we call this "buying a listing." These unscrupulous agents are a waste of your time because, inevitably, once they get your signature on a contract and their sign in your yard, they will begin "talking you down." And by then, you've lost your opportunity to capitalize on the market and get top dollar.

I continually advise both buyers and sellers to be diligent. Spend time with and interview an agent before you put your largest financial investment into his hands. At the end of the day, the home searching or marketing an agent does (or does not do) might be important, but the counsel he provides throughout the transaction is critical. *That counsel is only helpful if you listen to it.*

Every educated consumer should ask three questions about a potential agent:

1. "Am I confident that this agent is knowledgeable?"
2. "Do I have a level of trust in what she says?"
3. "Am I confident that she's working in my best interest?"

If the answer is yes, then listen to her advice. Her counsel, based on her expertise and experience, is her greatest value.

The 'Wiggle Room' Myth

Before ending this chapter, I would like to dispel the myth that you must build "wiggle room" into an offer (buyers) or an asking price (sellers). Here's why this practice is counter-productive

Let's look at buying. When I work with a buyer who develops an interest in a particular home, the first thing I do is run a comparative market analysis (CMA) on that exact property. You may be thinking, why run a CMA for a buyer? CMAs are not just for sellers; running a CMA for a buyer is the best way to avoid overpaying for a home.

If the property is priced too high—based on the CMA and my experience—we will certainly make an offer based on what the market is saying. But my team members have all had experienced buyers who, even when we tell them that the property is priced fairly or are even under-priced, still want to "low-ball" their initial offer. I will tell you that if a property is priced to the market, there is nothing wrong with offering close to list price, but then holding to that price.

One of my team members was excellent at this excellent at this strategy. She would recommend that the buyer come in with a strong initial offer, and she then would tell the other side, "My client has been educated about the market and sees the value in the home, which is why he is offering very close to list price. However, you should know that this is close to the top of what he will pay." Most sellers appreciated this candid approach and her transaction immediately started on a smoother playing field. Her goal was always win-win.

Of course, in a buyer's market, a buyer could take advantage of the situation, make a low-ball offer, and "steal the house." In my experience, however, the buyer will pay for it in the long run. In this situation, a seller who feels taken advantage of will typically say, "OK then, but I'm selling the house 'as is.' Don't even think about coming back to me with inspection issues because I'm not spending another dime." So it goes; each side tries to gain ground on the playing field and both lose in the end.

Let's look at the seller's side of this "wiggle room" now. Many sellers unequivocally believe that they must overprice their home so they have room to come down. This is a terrible strategy. Statistically, you will get the most money for your home when you price it close to what the market is indicating. In fact, even in a buyer's market, a well-priced home will often get multiple bids soon after being placed on the market.

As I counsel sellers, I believe the best strategy is two-fold. First, price your home to market, and second, hold to that price. If it is priced correctly, I can defend that price and tell the other side, "As you can see, my clients have priced their home very competitively, but you need to know they are not going to be coming down a lot."

In the United States and Canada, real estate transactions are one of the last bastions of "haggling." Our team sometimes works with buyers and sellers who won't feel good about a transaction unless they've "beaten" the other side. But the truth is that after guiding hundreds of transactions over the years, we can tell you that the best "deals" were win-win.

FROM THE CONSULTING TIMES:

Pricing Your Home

By ACRE® Merv Forney

PROPERTY AND HOMES ARE COMMODITIES, pure and simple. High demand and low supply drive prices higher and the asset becomes more liquid (easier to sell). Low demand and high supply drive prices lower and assets become less liquid (harder to sell). Market value is ultimately determined by what a buyer is willing to pay and a seller willing to take. I hear the following statements from consumers:

+ Well, I can't sell for less than my tax assessment!
+ My home is worth at least my appraised value!
+ My neighbor said...
+ My Mom told me...
+ The one down the street sold for...and my home is better...
+ Zillow says...

Let's take a look at the various pricing factors one at a time...

1. **Assessments:** The tax assessor compiles general data about about home sales in specific areas in a jurisdiction looking back at the last year. Yes, the last year. County records are incomplete, contain very little detail and are fraught with error. The assessor has no way to evaluate the quality of a property; condition, how well it is maintained, amenities, or any other qualitative measures. When was the last time an assessor visited your home to determine these things? Never! Markets change and can do so rather quickly. Demand drives market

value. The assessor doesn't have it. If anything, if you believe your assessment is too high, appeal it!

2. **Appraisals:** Appraisers have a little better handle on market value. They visit the property, take measurements, take pictures, note features and amenities, have opinions on quality and condition and are out in the market and have a pretty good idea of what's happening. They see lots of homes. They approach residential value from two perspectives, current cost to build (cost models that take into account lot, size of home and amenities) and comparable properties that have sold (usually in the last six months or so). The are also looking backward. Appraisers have algorithms and formulas for adjusting value based on comparisons of location, lot size, square footage, age, condition and amenities. Banks base their loans to buyers on an appraisal. But again, they are looking backward. A market value appraisal performed for a seller 3 to 6 months ago does not reflect current demand. So, we need to be careful about how we use it, if at all.

3. **Comparable Market Analysis (CMA):** This is the method used by most real estate agents. It is not only a comparison of similar properties that have sold (backwards looking in time), but also a comparison of similar properties currently on the market. We also look at location, condition, size, quality and amenities as well as time on market (an indicator of market condition). Knowledgeable, experienced agents will not provide a specific market value. Instead, they will provide an approximate range of potential value. We will also take into account buying patterns of consumers. For example, wood floors, upgraded cabinets and appliances, granite or stone counter tops, finished basements and home theaters are in strong demand. They are expected in certain price ranges. And, in a buyers market, homes that have these features will be the first to sell (everything else being equal, including price). So, if a home does not have these, a much lower price is what will attract a buyer. Adding these amenities will not necessarily allow you to set your price higher than comparable.

Adding these may, in fact, simply allow you to compete with other properties on the market that do have them. Bottom line: CMAs do not set market value...they are just estimates.

4. **Zillow:** New, exciting, cool, presents lots of information. Zillow bases their Zestimates on public records. See Assessments above. End of story for Zillow.

5. **Neighbors, family, friends et al:** These lovely trusted people have opinions. If they are not real estate agents or appraisers who have done the necessary homework, they don't have the data. Respect their opinion, but don't listen.

6. **All of the above (except #5):** All of these are helpful in estimating market value and we use all of them. We show potential clients how we use each of these to "triangulate," determining the most probable range of value. We use our market data studies, in general, to advise clients on what to expect. In a buyers market, sellers would be advised to set their price lower in the range. In a sellers market, higher in the range. Of course, competitiveness of the property plays a big factor as does the market price range sellers are in. Entry level properties have more potential buyers, high end properties have a significantly smaller pool of potential buyers. Of course, there are other personal factors to consider, such as how fast a seller needs to sell for whatever reason.

Sellers are not only competing with other sellers, they are competing with new home builders. In our current market, new home builders are offering huge incentives to buyers to move their inventory. These include all the bells and whistles mentioned above and/or CASH.

The conclusion? Pricing and presentation are everything in attracting buyers. Estimating market value is as much an art as it is a science. Be prepared to be logical and realistic above all else. Our job is to apply the art to the science and help sellers get the highest value that the market will provide.

Navigating Contracts, Disclosures, and Agency

Ignorance Is Not Bliss—It's the Stuff of Lawsuits

CONTRACTS SIGNED WITHOUT AN UNDERSTANDING of the implications, or an undisclosed problem with your home, can cause untold problems for you, at best holding up your closing and at worst, putting you in some very serious legal hot water. And the statement, "I didn't know" doesn't cut it in the vast majority of states. It is also vital to your interest to understand the laws of agency, or put another way, who represents (or doesn't represent) whom.

Contracts

Any discussion of contracts must be general in nature, since customs and/or requirements will vary from state to state. If you are working with an agent, no matter the method of compensation, you will need to sign a listing contract that spells out the required duties of each party, the amount and type of compensation due to the broker, and how it will be paid. Make sure that you understand what you are reading and signing—if your agent has to explain it three times, so be it.

In addition, whether you are represented by an agent or selling on your own, you'll need to complete various disclosure forms, which I'll discuss in the next section. Once you receive an offer, the documents will differ from state to state. In my home state of Massachusetts, we have a two-step process: an Offer to Purchase (with attendant contingencies), and then, ten days to two weeks later, a final Purchase and Sale Agreement. Most states have a one-step process. In Massachusetts, while the agent generally handles the offer, a real estate attorney will prepare and negotiate the final Purchase and Sale, and be responsible for closing the transaction. Most other states use title companies. Again, make sure that you fully understand the procedures in your state.

Disclosures

Many homeowners are not aware that in most states, you, as a homeowner, are required to understand what needs to be disclosed regarding your home. Failure to disclose is serious business!

It's one of the reasons that I caution homeowners to think twice about taking on the job of selling your home alone, or buying into a limited service arrangement where a harried licensee types in your house information for a fee. I can guarantee you that for the little money they are being paid, and the absence of any fiduciary representation, you won't get a careful review of the disclosures. And without representation, you are fully liable.

I am not exaggerating about the dangers of lack of disclosure. Let's look at a couple of real-life situation. One example was limited in its damages (since I, the listing agent, was responsible and paid for it), but the other resulted in very bad news for the unrepresented seller.

A few years back, I listed a home for a dear friend. I am generally very meticulous as to what I put into the MLS, but this time, I forgot to disclose that the home's water heater was rented. A buyer came along and put in an offer. Of course, during the home inspection, the rental status of this water heater was noticed. The buyer had made the offer believing that the water heater was part of the property. So I had to buy a new water heater! Even a full-service, experienced agent can make mistakes—but a good agent will make it right. Can you imagine how many more mistakes are made by "limited service" agents who aren't paid enough to be thorough, or worse, homeowners selling on their own?

I talked earlier about hiring referred professionals because they have accountability. In the above example I made a mistake, but because I'm a professional, I made the situation right. *There is value in accountability.*

Now, let's take a look at a more serious example of a lack of disclosure. About five years ago I brought some buyer clients to a home that was being sold "by owner" for a listed price of $425,000. Because my clients liked the home very much, and it was at the height of a seller's market with a tremendous shortage of inventory, they decided to put in an offer immediately. After a difficult negotiation with the seller, he finally accepted my buyers' offer.

At the home inspection a few days later, the inspector pointed out several water stains on the ceiling. Sure enough, when he went up to the attic, his moisture indicator showed that many of the boards were damp. Worse, he found evidence of earlier leaks. I was surprised that this issue wasn't disclosed, because roof leaks are a very easy condition for an inspector to discover. I was amazed that an owner, even one selling without representation, would not attend to, or at the very least disclose, a problem that he surely had knowledge of.

I got together with the seller later that day so that I could discuss the inspection. The seller claimed to have no knowledge of any roof leaks. I found that hard to believe, but I took him at his word. What really blew me away was that he refused to fix the leaks. The seller said, "Look, if they want the house, they will have to fix the roof themselves. If they don't want to, that's fine—I have a line of buyers behind them."

I replied, "You do understand that you are required now to disclose this issue to every subsequent buyer for your property." He smirked and said, "Yeah, right. Like in this market I'm going to have any trouble finding another buyer." I could tell that he wasn't taking what I was saying very seriously. And my buyers weren't about to pay for the roof repairs. The seller returned their deposit and I found my buyers another home.

If the next buyer had been unrepresented and naïve enough to buy the home without a good home inspection, perhaps this seller could have gotten away with selling his property without disclosing the roof leak. However, he would have had some serious legal liability once the property closed and the first heavy rains came. After all, it wouldn't take much investigation to find out about the existence of my buyers—the seller had bragged to all his neighbors about how he'd sold his house to my buyers the first day.

As it happened, the next interested buyers were also represented. The first question their buyer agent asked was, "How come your house is back on the market?" The seller was forced to say, "Oh, there's a minor leak in the roof and the buyers got all freaked out—

but the leak is very minor." Now the red flag was up—the buyers and their agent began to wonder what else this seller had not disclosed. They walked away without even putting in an offer.

Had the seller done the repairs (he did consider them minor) at the beginning, or, at the very least, disclosed the condition—which, after my buyers' inspection report, he could no longer deny knowing about—he probably would have sold his property to these subsequent buyers. But, because of his ignorance of the law and real estate practice and, worse, his arrogance when the facts were explained to him, his property languished on the market for three months. He finally hired an agent who told him on no uncertain terms that he'd better fix the roof or disclose the problem if he wanted her to market his listing. He ended up fixing the roof and selling his property for $375,000—a $50,000 loss that could have been avoided by a $500 repair or a disclosure of the condition, which would have cost him nothing!

This is a perfect example of the problems that sellers run into when they try to negotiate and navigate the process on their own. We agents do real estate for a living: we know what to look for and what questions to ask. The seller figured that he had a property to sell in a hot market, so he could avoid repairing his roof or even disclosing that a problem existed.

Most real estate professionals will nip the issue in the bud by having the seller fill out a Seller's Disclosure of Property Condition that asks the seller about any issues with all major mechanical and structural issues in the home. In fact, a Seller's Disclosure is required in many states.

Should You Do a Pre-Inspection?

When the market slowed down, I started recommending that our sellers consider having an inspection before listing their property. There are pluses and minuses of doing a pre-inspection. Clearly, whatever is discovered will have to be attended to or disclosed. Most buyers will have their own inspection anyway, but the benefit is that any items discovered can be addressed without pressure. In a slower market, I believe that a pre-inspection report, sitting on the table with the feature sheets, gives a prospective buyer a good feeling about the house and trust in the seller—and, hopefully, a competitive edge.

Environmental Disclosures

As a homeowner, you are expected to have knowledge of sewer regulations, the Lead Paint Law, radon, mold, and carbon monoxide. Yes, the list just keeps growing and unless real estate is your full-time job, it is difficult to keep up to date on laws and disclosure.

If you don't have a listing agent representing you, consider hiring a real estate consultant to review the necessary forms and disclosures your state requires. If you can't find a consultant in your area, even though it will generally cost more, make sure you confer with a real estate attorney.

Agency

I've saved this "big enchilada" for last. I'm passionate about agency because I've seen too many consumers get taken to the cleaners financially after making erroneous assumptions that the agent they were working with was representing them. In fact, the agent was representing the other side, or was representing no one.

If you haven't bought or sold a home in the last few years, you may not be up-to-date on the changes in agency law. Agency (representation) is one of the most misunderstood topics in real estate, not only by buyers but also by sellers.

It's always been important for buyers to understand agency because until buyer representation became common, almost every agent was really working for the seller. As Ken Deshaies and I discussed in our book, *How To Make Your Realtor® Get You the Best Deal: Massachusetts Edition*, various states began requiring agency disclosures because buyers were often not aware that "their agent" was actually working for the seller.

I have always been a stickler about each party having its own representation. I can't begin to estimate the number of consumers I've met with who've been royally screwed because they did not have representation. In fact, when I'm the listing agent on a property and a buyer calls me directly to see it, I always ask them if he has an agent, and if he says no, I encourage him to get one. If he insists on seeing the home with me, I say, "I will show you the house—but understand that I am representing the seller, so please don't say anything to me that you wouldn't say directly to the seller."

When I meet the buyer at the house, I'll (as required by Massachusetts law) hand him a Consumer-Licensee Disclosure stating in writing that I am working for the seller. Before he signs it, I "read" him what I jokingly refer to as his Miranda Rights in Real Estate, "You have the right to your own representation. Without representation, anything you say can and will be used against you. If you don't have representation and want it, I can refer you to someone…."

Most agents think I go a little overboard on this, especially since I could "double-end" the deal by having the buyers buy directly with me. But I believe very strongly that consumers are best served when each side has an agent representing their interests.

With or without my encouragement, buyer agency is not going away. The most educated and qualified buyers (the ones you want as a seller) increasingly demand their own representation, and all indications are that this trend will continue.

If you're a seller, do trust me on one thing—*buyers with their own representation should be welcomed, not feared!* Buyers who have their own representation are much easier to do business with than those who don't. Contrary to popular opinion, a buyer with her own agent is less likely to pick apart your home or make unreasonable demands. The reason is simple: a represented buyer has usually been educated about the buying process by her agent, and more likely to have been schooled on fair market value. As a listing agent, my experience is that buyers who make low-ball offers, make excessive demands, and pick the house apart during inspection usually have no representation. Without an agent working in their interest, these buyers often overreach because they're "on their own."

For sellers today, the widespread practice of buyer agency has changed the rules. Today, sellers need to be as cautious about what they discuss with agents who are not under contract to represent them as buyers should be. Unfortunately, most agents don't tell sellers that the rules have changed.

Let's take a look at the familiar practice of prospective sellers asking several agents in for a listing appointment and discussing with each the price they need and want for their home. It's not that I have a problem with sellers interviewing agents—it's prudent for both sellers and buyers to take the time to interview agents before hiring one.

But the discussion of a seller's wants, needs, and motivations with agents who are not under contract to represent them poses a problem.

Before the widespread practice of buyer agency, a seller could have several agents in and hire only one, knowing that the others would still be "working for them" and would not use whatever was discussed against them. But this is no longer the case. Today, once the seller chooses one agent, the agents who are *not* chosen could enter into a buyer agency contract with prospective buyers. If a buyer-client of one of those agents happens to be interested in that particular home, the agent is free to share with their buyers anything that the seller said during the listing appointment!

This is why, over the last year or so, my team has stopped the practice of preparing a market analysis up-front with a seller who is unknown to us. Now, when a seller calls me to " come look at my house," I tell them upfront, "Mr. and Mrs. Seller, my partner and I would be pleased to come over and discuss with you how we market homes and the general housing market. However, to protect your interests, we'll only discuss your specific pricing needs and reasons for selling once we're under contract to represent you."

Most sellers are taken aback by this statement because they have almost never heard this from any other agent. Just as with buyers, it's like reading them their "Miranda Rights": "Please understand that until you sign a contract, anything you say to an agent may be repeated to a buyer who might be interested in your home. I would advise you to not talk about your wants, needs, or the specific pricing of your home with any agent, until they are under contract to represent you."

Negotiating the Deal

The Best Real Estate Transactions Are Win-Win

THERE ARE TONS OF BOOKS already written about successful negotiating so this will be a short chapter. But don't let brevity fool you into thinking that negotiating a real estate offer is either unimportant or something that can be done successfully by anyone. On the contrary, as I've said earlier, if you are going to hire a real estate professional for just two things— negotiating is one of them (troubleshooting the transaction is the other one and the subject of the next chapter), do so here.

The successful negotiation of offers is a skill that is definitely honed with practice. It involves knowledge of the process, dates, and terms, as well as price. It requires a solid understanding of what is and what is not reasonable regarding the timing involved for an inspection, the language and dates regarding the buyer's loan commitment, and what contingencies are not in the seller's best interest. As we agents often say, "It's not the dollars but the terms that can kill you."

Successful negotiations also involve an ability to stay objective on your largest financial asset—a home that you may have put years of love into. This has nothing to do with talent or skill. I've seen many hard-nosed attorneys totally lose their cool when trying to entertain and negotiate offers on their own homes. For the record, I consider myself an expert negotiator for my clients, yet when it came time to sell my own home, I turned into the classic outraged seller, "What do you mean they only offered $_____. Don't they appreciate my home? Tell them to go take a walk!"

There's an old saying that any attorney who'd represent themselves has a fool for a client. It's no different in real estate and why most agents have a colleague negotiate offers on their own homes.

Negotiation of offers is absolutely where sellers going it alone often either give the store away or blow a deal that could have been successfully negotiated by not letting their emotions take over.

If you are either going it alone or, as can sometimes happen, you have found a buyer on your own without putting your house "on the market," don't let an inflexible commission system keep you from getting help in the critical area of negotiating. Many real estate consultants can provide expert negotiating for an hourly fee capped at whatever number of hours you're comfortable with. This is a great option when you don't want or need any marketing assistance. *Wow, I've found my own buyer — now, what do I do?*

Assessing Your Priorities

Even when you hire a professional to negotiate any offers on your home, you still have some homework to do.

Assess your priorities before you ever put your house on the market. Think through what's important to you when you are not in the heat of the moment. Ask yourself these questions:

- ✦ What terms of this sale are most important to me?
- ✦ How important is the ultimate sales price versus speed of sale?
- ✦ What is the small stuff that I will not sweat?
- ✦ What is a deal breaker for me?

Sellers can often "trade" something that is not important to them (like appliances) for something that is important (like a higher price).

The 'Have-No-Regrets' Exercise

Regarding a sales price, you might find it helpful (again, before you ever get an offer) to do the following exercise. Come up with the lowest sale price that you believe you could/would accept. Then test that price by thinking through a scenario where a buyer makes an offer on your property and you counter with this final figure and say, "Take it or leave it—this is the lowest I will go." Then think through two different outcomes:

1. The buyer accepts your final offer. Will you be happy because you sold your house at a price you can live with, or start

thinking to yourself that you should have made that final "drop dead" price higher. If you would have second thoughts, that final price wasn't the right one.

2. The buyer rejects your counter-offer and moves on. Will you be disappointed but know that you couldn't have gone lower, or start thinking to yourself that you shouldn't have held out for such a high price. If you think you should not have held out, that "drop dead" price wasn't right.

I have buyers do the same exercise, only in reverse: come up with a price that is the highest that they think they can pay for a house they are interested in. Test that dollar figure by thinking through what they might feel if the seller either accepted or rejected their offer.

I call this the "Have-No-Regrets" exercise, because when it comes to real estate negotiations, the best deal is the one that you have no regrets about when all is said and done.

In the End, Make It a Win-Win

As in most fields, real estate negotiations are the best when each side feels they have given something but gotten something in return. My colleague and friend Ken Deshaies said it perfectly in his book, *Get the Best Deal When Selling Your Home*:

> The vast majority of real estate deals, when both sides are repre-sented, should come down to what is fair. It should end up being a win-win situation, where everyone feels satisfied with the deal. We have all dealt with buyers who "want a deal" and who are unwilling to pay fair market value for any property. They want to steal it, to stick a knife in the seller's back and then twist it. They are only looking for someone who is vulnerable and has to sell at any price. We usually send away buyers like this.

It is true some deals are made like this. We have found properties on the verge of foreclosure, or where sellers have to make a quick sale to save themselves from bankruptcy. We have not hesitated to get one of our buyers into such a deal. But your Realtor® is there to protect you from buyers who take the attitude that they can only be happy if they have "screwed" the seller. This attitude is really just corruptive of the whole process of real estate.

Troubleshooting the Transaction

Nothing Else Matters if the Deal Doesn't Close

IF YOU'RE LIKE MOST CONSUMERS that I speak with, you might believe that the most difficult part of getting a home sold is putting it on the market and finding a buyer. But those of us who practice real estate for a living will tell you that the crucial stage is *after* you have a signed offer. From "contract to close" is when a good listing agent plays the role of a quarterback, directing all the activities on the field and doing her utmost to execute a winning game plan, all the way to a smooth and successful closing.

The reason most sellers focus on the period up to getting an offer is because that is when the visible work is being done. Preparing the home for market and the flurry of marketing activities and materials produced to get the word out get all the attention. A quality agent's most important work is quietly done behind the scenes after the offer is accepted. It's kind of like an iceberg: the visible part above the water is actually a very small part. What lies below the surface (where the sharks are) is the work that will make all the difference between whether you have a smooth transaction that closes on time, a myriad of problems, or a transaction that falls apart.

From acceptance of the offer to close, the "devil is in the details." It's the attention to those details that separates the boys from the men and the girls from the women. Here's a look at a small sampling of items that need to be attended to and monitored.

+ Have the buyers applied for their loan as specified in the offer, or are they still checking out lenders?

+ Are the issues raised at inspection reasonable, or is the buyer trying to renegotiate the sale?

- If the buyer has a home to sell, is someone keeping tabs on that other home's status?

- Has the appraisal been ordered in a timely manner?

- If the appraisal comes in low, will there be someone with the knowledge of the market to make a case to the buyer's lender?

- Are certain obligations that are required for closing—fixing issues raised at inspection, smoke detector and carbon monoxide certificates, and water and oil readings—being attended to?

- Is someone "riding herd" on the buyer's commitment and down payment to make sure they'll be in place by the date agreed?

These are just some examples of issues that, while seemingly small, can blow up a transaction late in the process and force a seller to start all over again, putting his house back on the market. If the seller has already scheduled a closing on his next home and needs the funds on this one in order to close, a disaster is in the making!

Riding herd on these issues is not difficult but it does require time and attention to the details, which is not an easy task unless you are familiar with the process and selling a house is your only job. This is why I list *troubleshooting the transaction* as one of the four big potholes in selling a home and why a seller would be well-advised to get help from a professional.

Having a quality listing agent is still no guarantee that problems won't arise. I wrote the following in the selling section on my team's website:

Selling your home is like taking an airline flight across the country. When you start on your trip, you have no idea how the trip will go. Neither does the pilot! You could run into turbulence, or you could have a smooth flight and land on time. Certainly, the pilot will try to use his or her experience to navigate around storms and go for the smoothest flight plan, but if they're honest, they can't promise a turbulence-free trip. Their job is to get you to your destination in the least time and with the least aggravation while keeping you informed throughout the trip.

As your real estate consultants, we see ourselves as the pilot of your plane. Our job is to assist you in getting your home sold for the most money, in the least time, with the least aggravation. We can't promise you no turbulence, but we can promise that we will utilize our experience and expertise to take you on the smoothest flight that we can. And if we do hit turbulence, we won't bail out on you. We'll be your teammates throughout the flight until we get you safely to your destination.

Over the years, I've spoken with many sellers who are trying to sell on their own, who tell me that when the time comes, "my attorney will attend to that stuff." I have the highest respect for quality attorneys and I count several as good friends, but just as I don't practice law, attorneys are generally not full-time Realtors® (if they're doing real estate full-time, you have to wonder about the health of their law practice). An attorney is not a good party to depend on to keep an eye out for all the real estate details that must be monitored—that is not what they do. Troubleshooting transactions is what Realtors® do. An experienced agent is very good at anticipating the inevitable potholes along the way and assuring those problems are resolved so they don't blow up transactions.

You, as a seller, might have a relatively simple transaction, have everything go as planned, and close with success. You may not need any help as long as there are no issues. The problem is that most issues don't raise their ugly heads until you're well along in the process. It's like the question, "Do you need fire insurance?" The answer is no, until you have a fire. As smart consumers, we buy insurance so we have the peace of mind to know that if we have a fire, we have the means to deal with it. It's the same with your transaction. Paying a good real estate consultant to oversee the transaction is a small price for the security of knowing that you'll be spared "surprises" late in the game. Many real estate consultants can provide this assistance for a very reasonable fee; you can find one at www.TheConsultingTimes.com/find (And if you, or someone you know, is in the real estate business and would like to get out of the commission trap, you'll find information on the ACRE® training and certification program at www.ACREcourse.com).

Conclusion

CONGRATULATIONS! You're now among the most educated non-professionals in the country about how real estate does and does not work, and how to get professional help without spending a fortune.

I hope you've found our journey together useful, and that you'll take this powerful new knowledge and use it to make the best deal you can when buying or selling, or thinking about the next steps to take with a property you own: a deal that is fair for the seller, the buyer, and the people who provide both parties with professional advice and counsel.

If you choose to work with an ACRE®, you can be proud, knowing that you're helping to create a whole new, and much more customer-friendly, model of doing real estate. I wish you well!

If you have feedback on your experiences, positive or negative, we'd like to hear them. Please contact us at council@theconsultingtimes. com and tell us how it's going.

If you're a real estate professional interested in more information on the Accredited Consultant in Real Estate® (ACRE) Training and Certification Program, please visit www.TheConsultingTimes.com and/or www.ACREcourse.com.

If you're a consumer who would like to learn more about real estate consulting, please visit www.MyREConsultants.com. And if you'd like to find an ACRE® in your area, visit www.TheConsultingTimes. com/find.

Both consumers and professionals are welcome to view our consulting videos at www.ACREonYouTube.com.

Questions? Contact council@theconsultingtimes.com.

You can contact the author directly at: mollie@molliew.com or at 508-294-0106 (US Eastern Time)

Index

attorneys

online 9, 49, 60
open house worth the 32

S

Sambrotto, Colby 70
Sichelman, Lew 69
Stuart, Ron ix, 81

T

Taylor, Heather Jones 29
technology 47, 54, 55, 56, 59, 68. *See also* Internet
online/Internet 59, 60, 87
Tuccillo, John 48

U

USA Today 60, 70, 71

W

Wallace, Bob 81
Walmart 100
WebMD.com 51
websites
craigslist.com 5
ForSaleByOwner.com 70
MDChoice.com 51
RebateReps.com 21
WebMD.com 51
ACREonYouTube.com 93, 138
TheConsultingTimes.com/find 93, 135, 138
TheHomeConsultants.com 48
Zillow.com 52

Z

Zillow 52, 53, 59, 117, 119 *See also* websites

About the Author

MOLLIE WASSERMAN is a pioneer in the development of Real Estate Consulting—an innovative business model that puts the needs of the client first by paying real estate professionals for their consulting expertise, whether or not a sale is appropriate

Throughout her real estate career, Mollie has always loved to play matchmaker—identifying people's needs and finding just the right products or services to match them. With her unique marketing talents and outgoing personality, she has successfully represented hundreds of buyers and sellers.

She has been at the forefront of real estate technology from the beginning of her real estate career. Her first website, MollieW.com (now TheHomeConsultants.com) went live in March of 1996. It has been featured in Banker & Tradesman, Forbes.com, Money.com, and the magazine for the National Association of Realtors®. In 1998, Intel profiled her as "the agent of the future" in its research paper on the transformation of the real estate industry.

Mollie is the founder of the Accredited Consultant in Real Estate (ACRE®) Training and Certification Program. Along with the other members of the ACRE® Council LLC Board of Advisors she developed an online Training and Certification Program launched in November of 2006, which guides real estate professional in implementing the consulting model in their own practice. Successful completion of this course leads to certification as an Accredited Consultant in Real Estate® (ACRE).

Born in Florida and raised in Texas,. Mollie attended school in Florida, Pennsylvania, and Mississippi before settling in the Boston area in 1979. She and her husband Steve live in Framingham,

Massachusetts with their two sons, Jeff and Dan, and a very cute Cavalier King Charles Spaniel named Kirby.

Mollie holds a Bachelor of Arts in mass communications from the University of Southern Mississippi and a Master of Business Administration with a concentration in marketing from Northeastern University.

She has achieved considerable distinction in her 15-year real estate career, earning recognition as an Accredited Buyer Representative (ABR), an e-PRO 500 (Select 50) Certified Internet Professional, an iSucceed Mentor, and one of only 200 Cyberstars™ around the world: an elite group of Realtors® who have generated a significant portion of their business through the use of current technology. A believer in continuing education, she has taken many advanced courses and holds a broker's license. She is also the co-author of *How to Make Your Realtor® Get You the Best Deal*—Massachusetts Edition.

In her free time, she enjoys cooking with Jeff, playing guitar with Dan, and rooting for her beloved Red Sox, Celtics, and Patriots.

CPSIA information can be obtained
at www.ICGtesting.com
Printed in the USA
BVOW11s0216090416

443601BV00020B/151/P